Keaun:

Allen Cute!.

Lou

02.08.16

CUTTING THE GORDIAN KNOT: UNDERSTANDING INVESTING
IN STOCKS, BONDS, AND MUTUAL FUNDS

A. A. NEESE
CPA, MBA, MS

Noble House
Baltimore, Maryland

CUTTING THE GORDIAN KNOT:
UNDERSTANDING INVESTING
IN STOCKS, BONDS, AND MUTUAL FUNDS

Library of Congress
Cataloging in Publication Data
ISBN 1-56167-496-6

Library of Congress Card Catalog Number:
99-60694

Cover illustration by Raymond Pomerico II

Published by

8019 Belair Road, Suite 10
Baltimore, Maryland 21236

Manufactured in the United States of America

DEDICATION

This book is dedicated to the members of my family who, each in his or her own way, empowered me to complete this work—my wife Deborah for her understanding; my brother Gordon for his encouragement; my mother Jean for her love of words; and my father Lon for his love of numbers.

THE LEGEND OF THE GORDIAN KNOT

In Greek legend, the Gordian knot was the name given to an intricate knot used by Gordius to lash his oxcart to a pole. Gordius, a poor peasant, arrived by oxcart with his wife in a public square of Phrygia, which is now part of Turkey.

An oracle had decreed that the future king would come riding in a wagon. Seeing Gordius, the people made him their king. In gratitude, Gordius dedicated his oxcart to Zeus, the righteous governor of the ancient world, tying it up with a particularly complex knot. An oracle foretold that whoever untied the knot would rule all of Asia.

According to a later legend, in 333 B.C., Alexander the Great severed the knot with his sword. From that day to this, "cutting the Gordian knot" has meant solving a difficult problem.

CONTENTS

FIGURES AND TABLES

AUTHOR'S DISCLAIMER

I have researched carefully the information, investment approaches and examples contained in this book in an attempt to ensure their accuracy. Nevertheless, I am unable to assume responsibility for any errors, omissions or inconsistencies.

Each of you should exercise your good judgment and/or consult an appropriate expert before adopting any of the approaches or applying any of the advice contained herein. I will respond gladly to individual questions or comments on the Web site: www.gordianknot.org.

I have referred to a number of people, companies, and organizations in this book. In no case was any disparagement intended.

1

Using This Book

If you are interested in investing, you are interested in making money. It could be for making a down payment on a home, financing your child's college education, or securing a comfortable retirement. But investing is inherently risky. In addition to the inherent risk, a day seldom goes by without the media trumpeting in recondite jargon the latest in a long litany of financial scandals and debacles. These events range from rogue stockbrokers, insurance agents and securities traders abusing the trust placed in them to entire regions of the globe—the most recent example dubbed "Asian contagion"—teetering on the brink of a financial meltdown that threatens the health of the U.S. economy. At the same time, the investment community bombards us at a dizzying rate with offers for increasingly sophisticated financial products and services through the telephone, television, radio, Internet and mail.

How do we avoid being taken for a ride? How do we sort out all these products and services and make informed choices? By trusting in luck? By resigning ourselves to ignorance and trusting solely in others? Or by learning enough about investing to deal effectively with the investment community?

The answer that I advocate is to cut with the sword of knowledge the Gordian knot of understanding investing. When it comes to matters as important as our financial goals and security, why go head to head with the sales side of the investment community with both hands tied behind our backs? The harsh reality is that we become sitting ducks for unscrupulous operators if we shirk this responsibility. Understanding investing takes some effort; but, after all, our financial health is at stake. The case for understanding investing has never been stronger. The American workplace has undergone a sea change in the last 15 years. The corporate model of lifetime employment that our parents knew has been replaced by outsourcing, contract employees, leased workforces and frequent job-hopping. This has sounded the death knell for most company pension plans that promised a guaranteed living wage for retirees in exchange for a lifetime of loyalty to one employer. Investing for a comfortable retirement income is the single greatest financial challenge that most of us will ever face. There are presently among us 76 million Americans who will reach retirement age by 2016. Many of them will suffer greatly diminished standards of living if they fail to live frugally and invest like mad between now and then.

At the same time, funding for federal, state and local safety nets, which historically cushioned the less fortunate, is being slashed in response to an erosion of altruism on the part of the electorate. Consider for a moment the 1.4 million U.S. bankruptcy filings in 1997, 96% of which were individual, or the visible homeless in your nearest large city. The U.S. Small Business Administration projects that the highest near-term job growth for all small businesses will be in the areas of debt collection and credit reporting. It expects employment in these two areas to grow from 1.74 million in 1994 to 2.93 million in 2005.

I have written this book for adults who are serious about increasing their financial IQ in order to deal effectively with the investment community. It covers the subjects that make up the investing body of knowledge at an understandable level. A dash of humor has been tossed in here and there as an antidote for the tedium inherent in these subjects for those of you who find numbers less than inviting. While there are a number of numerical calculations in this book, I have written the text so that performing them is not necessary to acquiring a full understanding of the contents. Of course, if you are inclined to perform them, please do so.

I cannot promise that *Cutting the Gordian Knot: Understanding Investing* will make you an expert on investing. I can promise it will increase both your financial literacy and numeracy and give you the tools to deal more effectively with the investment community. This book is divided into three building blocks; the first and second can be either read or omitted based on your knowledge and interest level. The three building blocks are shown in Table 1-1.

Table 1-1   Building Blocks

Contents	Chapters
1. Definitions and underlying numerical and conceptual features of investing	2, 3 & 4
2. Descriptions of the range of asset classes and investment professionals	5, 6, 7, 8 & 9
3. Practical application with case studies	10, 11, 12, 13 & 14

Certain words and phrases that are part of investing jargon appear in bold-faced type and are defined economically in a glossary. Names, organizations and companies are included in an index. Additionally, figures, tables and formulae are provided to illustrate and clarify key points.

I will touch on a large number of investing, tax and financial-planning issues. Each reader's financial profile is unique. Therefore, I urge you to follow this simple rule: If you don't fully—and I mean fully—understand something, get competent, impartial advice before placing your hard-earned money at risk.

2

INVESTING

SAVING COMES FIRST

Investing does not occur in a vacuum. It is only possible if you save money. This is really a behavioral issue for each of us. Our society places great emphasis on conspicuous consumption, and we Americans are among the least patient people on the planet when it comes to lifestyle choices. We also rank among the lowest of developed nations when it comes to saving as a percentage of our annual after-tax incomes. According to a Federal Reserve Bank's measure of personal savings that includes home ownership, Americans save less than 7%, which is well below the nearly 12% savings rate of Japan and lower than that of most industrialized European countries.

Saving requires us to maintain discipline over our spending habits and set aside money on a regular basis. It also requires us to control the urge to spend large, unplanned amounts of money that break the budget despite the great joy or instant status these purchases promise. Saving is no different from many other learned behaviors that we master as responsible adolescents and adults—studying hard, eating healthy foods, or making one more sales call each day. It takes conviction and effort to achieve meaningful results. "No pain, no gain"—as athletes are given to say—applies equally to the behavior of saving.

If you have children, the behavior of saving can be taught to them at an early age. Weekly allowances help children develop an awareness of money and the need to set aside some part each week for larger, future purchases. Additionally, opening a brokerage or savings account in a child's name and reviewing the monthly statement together can help to instill the saving habit.

I have found that showing teenagers the monthly household bills can be a real eye-opener. This is especially true in the areas of automobile payments, fuel, maintenance and insurance. It also can motivate them to begin saving for their first car at an early age, if they see just how much money they will need to own and operate it. The National Center for Financial Education in San Diego, California (Web site: www.ncfe.org) has been a pioneer in this area and sells a wide variety of materials and aids for teaching children about personal finance.

INVESTING DEFINED

If you have mastered the behavior of saving, you are in a position to begin accumulating **capital** for investing. Investing is a rational and systematic process with a high and reasonable expectation of gain that seeks to produce capital growth, income or both through the ownership of **assets**. This high and reasonable expectation of gain distinguishes investing from **speculating**, gambling and playing the lottery, which are based on chance not reason. Investing is further distinguished from speculating by its time frame. Investing is usually done over periods ranging from several to many years with fewer transactions and longer asset holding periods.

The primary motivation for investing is to achieve a set of financial goals at some time in the future. These goals can include large, planned expenditures such as the purchase of a home, a child's college education, maintenance of a comfortable standard of living during retirement, or simply the accumulation of wealth to leave to loved ones or to charity. Without a rational and systematic investment plan, it is less likely you will achieve these financial goals.

WHAT SHOULD YOU INVEST IN?

Think of all the people you have known who have owned things as diverse as classic American cars, antique furniture, baseball cards, rare coins, works of art and vacation homes. These are called assets and each of them has unique characteristics and risks that determine its effectiveness as an investment. **Material** assets such as classic cars, antique furniture, rare coins and works of art are not income producing. They are also hard to value accurately because no two are identical in quality and condition. Finally, they are often **illiquid**, or difficult to convert to cash rapidly, which makes them riskier than more **liquid** investments such as securities listed on a **major exchange** for which an active and continuous market for buyers and sellers exists.

Real estate, including vacation homes, is also unique and hard to value accurately until a firm offer to purchase is received. Real estate is costly to buy and sell due to commissions and other costs of transfer that can easily range from 5 to 10% of the purchase price. Finally, it is not income producing unless it is converted to rental property. For these and other reasons, real estate is less liquid—and frequently riskier—than securities listed on a major exchange. Nevertheless, a well-located and reasonably priced principal residence can be a sound investment due in large measure to easily accessible **mortgage** money and U.S. tax laws. A mortgage is a loan that permits a homeowner to control a potentially appreciating asset with 20% or less of its purchase price. Our country has a long-standing and well-developed mortgage-lending industry with a wide variety of loan programs. Most lenders require your annual mortgage payments not to exceed 28% of your annual income before taxes.

Borrowing to purchase real estate—or any other asset—is called **leverage**. It can greatly magnify the return on your original investment if the property is sold later at a profit. This is due to the fact that the lender is not entitled to share in the gain of the home's value, but only to repayment of the remaining loan balance. The homeowner owns all the **equity** in the home and any increase in its value. The homeowner also assumes all the risk of loss in value and, in the event of such loss, still must repay the entire remaining loan balance upon sale. This illustrates the peril of borrowing money to purchase assets.

Just as importantly, U.S. tax law permits a homeowner to deduct mortgage interest and real-estate taxes paid from gross income. This amounts to a subsidy for homeowners of up to 39.6% of these expenses at current top federal income-tax rates. Additionally, a principal residence is one of the very few assets usually not subject to tax if it is sold for a profit or gain. These are enormous benefits and underpin to a large extent residential real-estate values.

In our current tax environment, a carefully selected and sensibly priced principal residence with an affordable mortgage can be a good investment; it deserves consideration as one of the assets acquired in your investment **portfolio**. The popularity of residential real estate has been enhanced further by the flexibility with which money can be raised by converting the equity in a property to cash. This can be accomplished by means of a tax-deductible **home-equity loan** and, more recently, a **reverse mortgage**, which applies to homeowners over 65 years old.

Despite the popularity, pride of ownership, tax advantages, and potential for profit of residential real estate, securities listed on a major exchange including stocks, bonds, mutual funds and annuities have become the assets of choice for building wealth. A recent analysis of governmental data by the *New York Times* reveals that at the end of September 1997, American households had more of their wealth invested in stocks than in their homes. This is a first in the last 30 years and is, of course, partly due to the surge in the U.S. stock markets over the past several years.

There are several advantages to securities. No other type of asset even comes close to the range of choices available with listed securities. In most cases, for a few thousand dollars or less, you can become an owner in businesses providing every imaginable product or service in every corner of the globe. Owners of securities have ready access to market prices in the local newspaper and the various on-line computer services. Additionally, they are protected to some degree by a well-developed body of laws and regulations that covers areas ranging from security-sales practices and mutual-fund performance reporting to corporate accounting methods. This body of laws and regulations is enforced effectively by the Securities and Exchange Commission (SEC) and the National Association of Securities Dealers (NASD), whose watchdog role helps to make the American securities markets the model for the world in terms of efficiency, disclosure and consumer protection. Listed securities are very liquid and can be bought and sold rapidly and cheaply, in most instances, due to the explosive growth of discount and on-line brokerage firms.

Finally, rating services, investment-house research, investor-oriented broadcasts and publications, Web sites, and quarterly and annual audited financial statements with comments to both shareholders and the SEC provide an enormous supply of current information about security issuers' financial performance and prospects. Much of this information is available not only in hard copy, but also on the various on-line computer services being marketed widely today.

As of April 1998, there were over 9,000 stocks and 12,000 debt instruments listed on major U.S. exchanges. These alone account for over 35% of the global market value of listed securities in a nation with only 5% of the world's population. In addition, nearly every other developed nation and many less-developed and emerging nations have active securities markets. Together these markets provide the public forum for buying and selling the securities of existing and new businesses. No wonder securities listed on national exchanges have become the most flexible and popular asset classes for small and large investors alike.

At some time in your life, you very likely will be entertained by people recounting tales of their investing successes in assets other than listed securities. In a very few of these cases, the investor probably possessed specialized knowledge that enabled him or her to succeed. But in a large number of these cases, the investor was most likely just plain lucky. It is also likely that investing tales, like fish and golf stories, are embellished greatly as time goes on. Additionally, it is human nature to minimize or conveniently forget those investments that "went south," or failed.

I have been involved personally and professionally in a host of investments including rental property, equipment leasing, oil and gas drilling, precious metals, classic automobiles, antique furniture and fine paintings. Although I have occasionally picked a winner with these assets, my track record is spotty at best. Importantly, on those occasions when I needed to raise cash in a hurry, these assets were difficult to sell rapidly and, in some cases, to sell at all. I am convinced that unless you possess considerable skill and knowledge in an alternative area of investments, you should concentrate on listed securities in building your investment portfolio.

3

NUMBERS

"If you can't express it in numbers, you don't know what you're talking about!" I started out in business as a freshly minted accountant hearing this timeworn homily from my boss. It suggests that numbers are the language of business; to a great extent this is true.

Imagine arriving in a foreign city where you could not understand the written and spoken language or even make sense of the road signs. That is precisely how most people feel about investing. If you happen to feel that way, don't worry! You are not alone in this sentiment.

A familiarity with the contents of this chapter will increase greatly your investing numeracy. If you are so inclined, grab a pencil and pad of paper, a financial calculator or your trusty laptop and follow along with the examples.

COMPOUND INTEREST

Interest is the rent that lenders charge borrowers for the use of money. It is important to understand how it is calculated. If you borrow $100 for 12 years at 6% annual **simple interest**, you would owe $172 at the end of the loan period. This consists of the original loan of $100 plus $6 per year of interest times 12 years, or $72.

If you borrow the same $100 for 12 years at 6% annual **compound interest**, you would owe $201 at the end of the loan period. This consists of the original loan of $100 plus 6% interest on the loan and accumulated interest each year, which amounts to $101. This difference of $29 (101 - 72 = 29) grows larger as the years increase. The power of compounding over a 24-year period is illustrated in Table 3-1.

Table 3-1 Loan Comparison

Simple versus Compound

($ Rounded)

End of Year No.	$100 6% Simple	$100 6% Compound
1	106	106
6	136	142
12	172	201
18	208	285
24	244	405

At the end of 24 years, you would owe $244 with a 6% simple-interest loan of $100 and $405 with a 6% compound-interest loan of the same amount. The power of annual compounding is what math mavens call rising, or **exponential**; simple interest, on the other hand, is straight line, or **linear**. Incidentally, and surprisingly, compounding monthly—or even daily—at 6% does not make much of a difference compared to annually. Notice the shape of the lines shown in Figure 3-1, which contains the same values as Table 3-1.

Figure 3-1

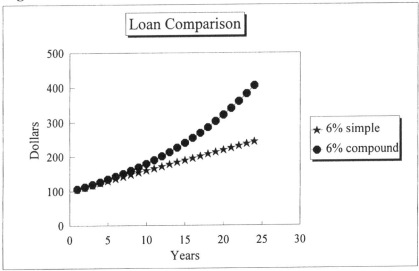

RULE OF 72

This handy rule makes use of the constant 72, which is derived from the compound-interest formula. It permits you to make a quick estimate of the annual compound rate needed to double your money over a given number of years. For example, the rate needed to double your money over 12 years is about 6%. This is arrived at by dividing the number of years into the constant 72 (72/12 = 6).

You can estimate just as easily the number of years over which your money will double if you use a given rate. For example, money invested at a rate of 9% will double in about 8 years. This is arrived at by dividing the rate into the constant 72 (72/9 = 8).

As you work and become familiar with this rule, you will be able to make more complex estimates. For example, $100 invested at a rate of 9% will triple in about 12 years. This is arrived at by first adjusting the constant 72 from doubling to tripling as follows: (3/2 x 72 = 108). Next, you divide the rate of 9% into the adjusted constant 108 to arrive at 12 years (108/9 = 12). *Voila!* Just that simple!

INFLATION

A period when prices of goods and services are rising overall is called inflation. This has been the case to varying degrees in the United States since World War II. Inflation reduces the purchasing power of money and motivates people to seek wage and salary increases. It also motivates people and firms to seek positive returns on capital such as interest, rent and profit to compensate for this loss of purchasing power.

Generally speaking, borrowers benefit at the expense of lenders because borrowers will pay back loans with future dollars, which are less valuable than those they received at the time of the loan. This is particularly punishing if the lender has no right to adjust the interest rate for unexpectedly high inflation. Adjustable, or floating-rate, debt was designed by lenders to adjust for unexpected inflation by linking the loan interest rate to some indicator that can reflect future inflation and is tamperproof.

The **consumer price index (CPI)** is calculated and published monthly by the federal government's Department of Labor Statistics. The calculation process employs over 300 pricing agents, who collect prices on some 90,000 items. The CPI is used often as an indicator of purchasing-power changes at the consumer level for purposes of adjusting wages and salaries for workers. Similarly, published interest rates paid to buyers at auctions of debt issued by the federal government are used often as indicators of current market interest rates for purposes of periodically adjusting rates on personal, business and mortgage loans.

Since changes in purchasing power play such an important role in analyzing interest and other investment returns, it is helpful to eliminate the effects of inflation and focus on the remainder. This remainder commonly is called the inflation-adjusted rate, or **real rate**. For example, a mortgage loan on which you pay 7% annual interest during a year in which the CPI rises 3% has a real rate of interest of 4% (7 - 3 = 4). If the CPI declines 2%, the real rate is 9% (7 - (-2) = 9). A prolonged decline in the CPI is called deflation. Deflation, which is increasingly possible in the United States based on 1998 economic indicators and events to date, favors lenders at the expense of borrowers.

Real rates are particularly meaningful when comparing interest rates and other investment returns over longer periods of time to see how they maintain purchasing power.

TIME VALUE OF MONEY

The time value of money is linked closely to money's diminishing purchasing power over time due to inflation. It provides a method for adjusting past, current and future receipts and payments of money to a constant purchasing-power basis.

If you were offered the receipt of $100 in ten years, you would be inclined to pay some lesser amount today to compensate for the ten-year wait. This lesser amount is called the **present value**. It is calculated by using the **discount formula**. If you accepted 6% as the annual compound rate to compensate for the loss of use of your money for this period, you would be satisfied to pay no more than about $56 today.

By the same token, if you paid someone $100 today in exchange for repayment in ten years at 6% annual compound interest, you would be satisfied with no less than about $179 then. This greater amount is called the **future value**. It is the **reciprocal** of the present value formula and is calculated by dividing the discount formula into one. Both of these formulae are shown in the glossary under future and present value, respectively.

Did you know that businesses exist that will purchase the future monthly payments from an out-of-court settlement for a lump sum of cash? There are also businesses that purchase multi-year lottery winnings for immediate cash. This practice is hardly new. Years ago, the ne'er-do-well offspring of moneyed European families began selling **anticipations** to financial firms that provided them immediate cash in exchange for their documented future inheritances. Believe me, such companies know exactly how to use the present value formula we just discussed.

TAXATION

All of us who live in America and earn income are subject to federal income taxes. In 1996, individuals paid $656 billion in federal income taxes, which was nearly four times the amount paid by corporations. This represented 42% of the federal government's income from all sources. Many of us live in states that also impose their own income taxes. Income includes wages, salaries and profits from businesses and most types of investments on a global basis. Taxable income is the sum of all forms of income less the host of exemptions, deductions and credits contained in the current U.S. tax law.

There is no economically or socially sound rationale for many of our tax laws. They are the result of special-interest groups lobbying federal lawmakers. As a result, the Internal Revenue Service (IRS) tax code has become mind-numbingly complex for both individuals and businesses. According to the U.S. Congress, the IRS code alone runs 9,471 pages. Additionally, the regulations and interpretive rulings surrounding the tax code run some 91,824 pages. In contrast, the Holy Bible (Revised Standard Version), which contains both the Old and New Testaments, runs 1,290 pages.

This has led to a number of failed bills in Congress calling for sweeping tax simplification. Despite this, I believe that the current system will be reformed periodically in small ways and made more taxpayer-friendly, but will remain in place for the foreseeable future. As you continue reading this section, contemplate for a moment why the government requires so much of your income to run the country when for centuries God has run the entire world on tithes. Federal personal regular income-tax rates range from 15% to 39.6%. In addition, there are **alternative minimum tax (AMT)** rates of 26% or 28% to which a rapidly increasing number of people are subject who otherwise would be in the 15% bracket. Originally, AMT was designed to snare the superrich who paid little or no taxes through the use of elaborate tax-avoidance techniques not available to *hoi poloi* like you and me. Since the AMT threshold is not indexed for inflation, it is systematically lowered every year. It is estimated that by 2008 nearly 9 million taxpayers will be subject to AMT rates. Oh, well! That's what happens when our government uses an ax instead of a scalpel.

State personal income-tax rates range from zero to 10% depending on where you live. Income taxes reduce the return on most investments and are one of the important considerations when comparing returns from different types of assets. The U.S. income-tax laws contain a break for investors that imposes a lower tax on long-term gains in the price of securities than on income. This lower tax is called **capital gains** and requires that you hold a security for at least a year prior to its sale. The maximum federal capital-gains rate is 20%. Additionally, losses in the price of assets upon sale can be used to offset gains, which can make this tax break even more attractive.

Certain types of investments are not subject to federal income tax. These are called **tax-exempt**. Investments that are not subject to federal or state income tax are called **double tax-exempt**. In addition, investments that are not subject to federal, state or city income tax are called **triple tax-exempt**. Other types of investments are only subject to income tax when the income and profits are withdrawn at some time in the future. These are called **tax-deferred**. All other investments are **fully taxable** in the year when income or profit is paid to the taxpayer.

By the way, different asset classes may be treated differently under federal and, if applicable, state transfer-tax laws. Transfer-tax laws cover gifts made during your life and by your estate at death. Federal transfer-tax rates alone progress from 18% to 55% and can reduce dramatically your wealth in the hands of your heirs. Also, some tax-deferred retirement vehicles can have particularly punishing consequences in the absence of proper planning due to their unpaid income taxes.

I recognize this is no fun to think about. Mortality rarely is. However, if your lifetime gifts and expected estate combined exceed the **unified credit**, which in 1998 stands at $625,000 and is scheduled to rise in stages to $1 million by 2006, or you have significant retirement-account balances, you are a candidate for competent gift- and estate-tax advice. It can be enormously valuable in reducing the government's share of the wealth you worked so hard to accumulate. Your heirs will be especially thankful and remember you in the kindest light for your foresight and good planning. Provided the inheritance is sufficiently large, they even may be inclined to erect a small monument to your brilliance.

RULE OF 3S

The rule of 3s holds that over longer time horizons, all industries in a market economy tend to be dominated by three major competitors. Academic studies and compelling corroborative evidence exist to support the rule of 3s. The U.S. auto industry is an obvious example. Less obvious is the present tendency to reach three major competitors again as the auto industry moves from national to global in scope. The recently announced merger of Daimler-Benz and Chrysler is the first step toward this new order.

Obviously, in newer industries it takes some time for the rule of 3s to govern. A company whose market position enables it to repeal the rule of 3s can be an excellent investment. For instance, Microsoft's near monopoly in PC operating systems has enriched its shareholders enormously. At the same time, forces in our legal system militate against this dominance continuing indefinitely. The enforcer of the Sherman Antitrust Act, the U.S. Justice Department, may accelerate the effect of the rule of 3s.

RULE OF 5S

The rule of 5s—also called the 80/20 rule—is credited to an Italian economist named Vilfredo Pareto, who discovered certain patterns in economic events and behavior. The rule suggests that about 20% of all economic activities account for about 80% of the result. For example, if you are researching investments, there is more information available from all the many sources than any person can possibly digest working full-time every single day. About 20% of what you select to read or listen to will likely provide about 80% of the useful information.

The message here is to set priorities for your efforts and be selective in what you spend your valuable time doing. Experience and common sense will help you decide which sources of investment information are best suited to your needs and level of technical expertise.

DOUBLE TO GET EVEN

This simple rule serves as a constant reminder of the penalty for losing money in an investment. If you invest $100 in an asset and it declines to $50, your loss is 50% (50/100 = .5). However, to get back to even your asset must double, or rise in value 100% (50/50 = 1). The message here is to take losses in asset values very seriously and avoid them like the plague due to the sheer difficulty of recovering to even.

STATISTICS

Statistics is the science of collecting, classifying and interpreting information based on numbers. It is widely used in investing to describe the characteristics and behavior of market indicators, investment portfolios, asset classes and individual investments. Always bear in mind that most statistics by their very nature are backward-looking because they are based on historical information. Statistics can, however, provide investors with tools that have some predictive value, as long as history repeats itself to some degree.

Graphs, bar charts and pie diagrams are found frequently in financial writing and analysis. These visual aids can be used to show numerical observations, or data, at a single point in time or over longer periods at convenient intervals—monthly, quarterly, yearly or longer. An example of each of these is shown in Figure 3-2.

Figure 3-2

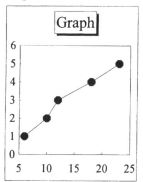 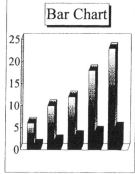 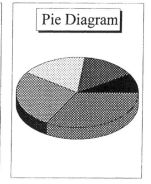

Since the advent of low-cost computers, large amounts of data can be cheaply and rapidly processed and summarized. A collection of numerical observations, or data, is called a population. One useful way to view a population is with the notion of a central value. This can be expressed in three ways:

1. The **arithmetic mean**, or average, which is the sum of all the values in a population divided by the number of population members.
2. The **median**, which is the middle value in a population that has been arranged from lowest to highest.
3. The **mode**, which is the most frequently appearing value(s) in a population.

Incidentally, the arithmetic mean, or average, is expressed frequently on a basis that gives greater weight to some members of a population than others. Remember how in high school or college the grade point average (GPA) assigned greater weight to your grade in quantum physics than in intramural water ballet? That's because the institution was using the **weighted-average** method to figure GPAs. In investing, averages are weighted frequently by dollars or time to make them more meaningful.

Another important feature of a population is the **variability**. It shows how much the members fluctuate around the population average. For the time being, we will work simply with the difference between the values of each member and the population average. This difference can be positive, negative or zero. Math whizzes among you take heart! I promise that later in this book we will calculate the estimated **standard deviation** as a more advanced expression of variability.

The data in Table 3-2 represent the average June prices of one ounce of gold on the London, U.K. Exchange in whole U.S. dollars from 1987 to 1997. Let's derive the statistical measures discussed above from these data.

The average price is $383. This is calculated by dividing $4,218 by 11 observations: (4,218/11 = 383). The median price is $372. This is the sixth, or middle, observation of 11 in the series arranged from low to high. The modes, or most frequent observations, are $341 and $367, which make this population **bimodal**.

The variability around the population average ranges from +$68 to -$42. This range is expressed in dollars and is called the **absolute** range, or **amplitude**. This range also can be expressed as a percentage of the population average: +$68 is +18% (+68/383 = +.18) and -$42 is -11% (-42/383 = -.11). This range is expressed in percentages and is called the **relative** range. The relative range can be helpful to maintaining a perspective when the data is expressed in very small or large numbers. For example, a 3/4% absolute increase in your adjustable-rate mortgage may seem small even if you were paying 6%. However, the relative increase is 12.5% (.75/6 = .125). That doesn't seem so small all of a sudden, does it? Similarly, a $1 billion drop in Bill Gates' personal fortune may seem catastrophic to us, but it only represents about 2.5% (1/40 = .025) of his $40 billion. Now, that wasn't so awful after all, was it?

The absolute variability of June gold prices on the London Exchange is shown on the bar graph in Figure 3-3. As you already know, statistics is backward-looking and has only limited application for predicting the future. As I sit here in March 1998, London gold prices are under $300 per ounce. This steady decline is due in part to low inflation expectations. Also, it is estimated that government central banks alone hold 35,000 tons of physical gold, which represents 14 years of current mine production. If they become sellers of gold, the price is likely to fall farther as we shall see in the section on supply and demand.

Table 3-2   London Gold
                        ($ Rounded)

June in Year	P Observed Price	A Average Price	V = P - A Variability of Price	Observed Price: Low to High
87	450	383	67	341
88	451	383	68	341
89	367	383	-16	367
90	370	383	-13	367
91	367	383	-16	370
92	341	383	-42	372
93	372	383	-11	385
94	386	383	3	386
95	388	383	5	388
96	385	383	2	450
97	341	383	-42	451
Total	4,218			

Figure 3-3

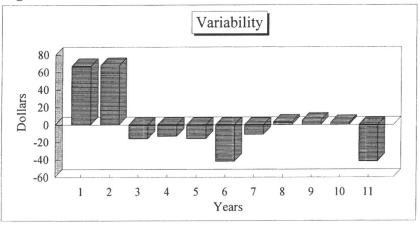

Another important statistical feature is the **correlation coefficient**. It shows the degree to which two variable quantities are systematically connected. This is a very useful measure in classifying assets according to their historical price movements relative to each other, economic influences, or the market as a whole in which they are traded. The measure of asset classes' movements relative to each other is called **cross-correlation**. Identifying the cross-correlation coefficients among asset classes based on historical rates of return can be a useful tool for investors.

Asset classes that have similar price movements over time are **positively correlated**. Asset classes that have opposite price movements over time are **negatively correlated**. Asset classes that have random, or unconnected, price movements over time are **uncorrelated**. These three correlation patterns are shown in Figure 3-4.

If this section on statistics whetted your appetite for the subject, I recommend reading *Statistics Without Tears* (Charles Scribner's Sons, 1981) by Derek Rowntree. It does a nice job of covering the rudiments.

Figure 3-4

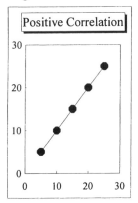 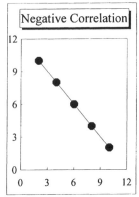 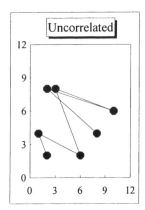

ERROR DETECTION BY 9S

This handy little trick has nothing to do with investing, but I couldn't resist including it here while we're in a mathematical frame of mind. Since our number system is based on 10, most slips of the pencil or keyboard can be tracked down easily with a little detective work.

A **slide error** occurs when you place the decimal point in the wrong place. For example, if you write a check for $140.00 and enter $14.00 in your check register, the error in your monthly reconciliation, assuming you reconcile your account—which I urge you to do now and then—will be $126.00 (140 - 14 = 126). This amount is evenly divisible by 9: (126/9 = 14).

A **transposition error** occurs when you reverse two digits in an amount. For example, if you deposit $1,521.00 in your bank account, and record it as $1,251.00, the error in your monthly reconciliation will be $270.00 (1,521 - 1,251 = 270). This amount is evenly divisible by 9: (270/9 = 30).

Once you see that your reconciliation is out of balance by an amount evenly divisible by 9, you know to look for slide- and transposition-error candidates. By the way, the culprit may be more than one error since multiple errors of these types still will be evenly divisible by 9. In our example above, the sum of both errors is $396.00 (126 + 270 = 396). $396.00 is also evenly divisible by 9: (396/9 = 44). If this helps you balance your accounts late some night, it was worth your time to read this section on error detection.

ACCOUNTING

If there was ever a subject the mere mention of which is guaranteed to make your eyes glaze over, accounting is it! Like statistics, it not only deals with historical events in wearisome detail, but also uses unfamiliar jargon and boatloads of numbers. Unfortunately, a nodding acquaintance with the financial statements of a business and the meaning of their contents is an important skill in making informed investment decisions. As you don armbands and a green eyeshade in preparation for this section on accounting, I pledge to make it as brief and painless as possible.

Accounting really can claim to be the language of business. It is divided into two distinct areas: **management accounting** and **financial accounting**. Management accounting deals with the information that is used to run a business profitably from the inside. It includes development and monitoring of sales goals, product-cost information, operating budgets and capital-spending plans. It is considered confidential and is limited to use by the directors, managers and supervisors of a business.

Financial accounting deals with the information that serves as the basis of the annual financial statements. These financial statements are presented to the outside constituencies of a business, which include lenders, suppliers, customers, governmental regulators and investors. Financial accounting is based on principles and standards that are designed to provide fairness, comparability and consistency of presentation. These principles and standards, which number in the hundreds, are called generally accepted accounting principles (GAAP). They are developed by the Financial Accounting Standards Board (FASB) and the American Institute of Certified Public Accountants (AICPA).

Despite its appearance of tidiness and precision, financial accounting often is based on estimates. For example, the future cost of fulfilling warranties on products or services delivered to customers is based on management's best estimate. Similarly, the future cost of restructuring or rightsizing a business to make it more efficient also is based on management's best estimate. The accounting recognition of this estimating process is called booking **reserves** and can be a potential source of distortion in the financial statements.

Additionally, GAAP permits choices in the treatment of certain accounting practices, which can produce different outcomes in the financial statements. For example, a business can choose among several methods for determining which product units were sold during the year and which remain on hand at year-end. These methods are called **cost-flow assumptions**. A business that chooses to value units sold at the most recent cost has elected last-in, first-out (LIFO). During a time period in which costs generally are rising, LIFO tends to reduce net income. Conversely, a business that chooses to value units sold at the oldest cost has elected first-in, first-out (FIFO). During a time period in which costs generally are rising, FIFO tends to increase net income. Once a method has been chosen, GAAP requires that it be disclosed and applied consistently from year to year. Incidentally, my personal favorite cost-flow assumption often is applied humorously to slow-moving retail goods. It is first-in, still-here (FISH) and speaks for itself.

Another accounting practice that can produce very different outcomes is the treatment of costs related to marketing to new customers. Conservative accountants argue that such costs should be classified immediately as expense, which reduces current profit. More aggressive accountants argue that such costs should be classified as assets and expensed in future years to match expenses more closely with revenues. The latter approach increases current profit and can distort the financial picture of the business if the revenues are recognized more rapidly than the expenses that produced them. This accounting treatment has led to some real debacles in financial reporting and investor confidence. Recently, Cendant Corp., a direct-marketing and franchising concern, announced it had engaged in delayed expense recognition and would restate downward its past and current years' profits. The stock price promptly **elevator shafted** and lost over $14 billion, or 46%, in a single trading day. Ouch! That smarts!

Finally, GAAP can be criticized for not reflecting in the financial statements the economic value of certain significant **intangible assets** of a business such as brand names, customer lists or the superior quality of its employees. Coca-Cola, the soft-drink seller, has an enormous economic asset in its trademark and global name recognition. Similarly, Intel, the chip and memory-circuit manufacturer, has great economic value in the skill of its engineering staff. Currently, GAAP simply is not able to assign objective values to assets like these, so they are excluded from the financial statements.

The exception to this exclusion may occur when a business is purchased at a price in excess of the value reflected in its financial statements. In this case, the financial statements of the surviving business may reflect a long-term asset called **goodwill**, which is a catchall for intangible assets. Incidentally, the collective wisdom of investors emphatically does recognize the enormous worth of these intangible assets. That is why the value in the marketplace of Coca-Cola and Intel stock bears no relationship to the value shown on their books. At December 31, 1997, the shares of Coca-Cola and Intel traded at over 26 and 6 times **book value**, respectively.

The notes to the financial statements of a business must disclose the significant accounting policies it follows. They can be an important source of information in analyzing a business. Most investors regard U.S. financial-accounting practices as setting the highest standard in the world. Despite ongoing efforts in the international accounting community, comprehensive, uniform international accounting and reporting standards do not exist today. However, the over eight hundred foreign companies listed on U.S. stock exchanges as of October 1, 1998 are subject to GAAP, which is a significant step in the direction of more transparent and uniform financial reporting.

There are three separate but related financial statements that are prepared by the management of a business. Before these financial statements are published, they are examined for compliance with GAAP by independent auditors. Independent auditors are Certified Public Accountants (CPAs) whose charge is to perform such tests and procedures as they deem necessary to render an opinion on the presentations contained in the three financial statements. This opinion is an integral part of the audited financial statements and carries great weight in the investment community.

Before we look at the three financial statements of a business, permit me to share with you a conceptual framework that I find helpful. Accounts and financial statements can be divided into two categories. One measures levels at a particular moment in time. The other measures flows over a stated period of time.

If I asked you how much fuel you presently had in the family car, you could determine this level accurately by reading the fuel gauge and reporting your answer in gallons. Let's say it reads ten gallons. If I then asked you to keep track of how much fuel you purchase in the next month, you could determine this flow accurately by keeping all your receipts and adding them up in gallons. Let's say you purchase 67 gallons during the next month. Now, if I asked you how much fuel you had consumed during the month, you could not determine this flow accurately because you would be missing a vital piece of information. Fuel available for consumption is the beginning level plus all purchases. Fuel consumption is fuel available for consumption less the ending level. So, you will have to read the fuel gauge at the end of the month to determine the ending level accurately. Let's say it reads six gallons at month's end. Then your fuel consumption would be 71 gallons. This calculation is shown in Table 3-3.

As you can see from this example, both levels and flows play a role in accounting. Accounts that measure levels always have a balance even though it may be zero (imagine reading the fuel gauge after running out of gas versus after filling it up). These are called permanent accounts. Accounts that measure flows are set to zero at the beginning of each new time period, so that only activity during that period is measured. These are called temporary accounts. All financial accounts can be divided into these two categories, as you will see in looking more closely at the three financial statements of a business.

Table 3-3   Fuel Consumption Aid

	Date	Gallons
Beginning level	02/01/98	10
Purchases	02/07/98	18
	02/15/98	17
	02/22/98	15
	02/27/98	17
Fuel available		77
Less: ending level	02/28/98	-6
Fuel consumption		71

The first of these three statements is the statement of assets and liabilities, or balance sheet, which shows things owned by the business (assets) in one column and claims on these assets by creditors and owners (liabilities and owners' equity) in another. These columns are necessarily equal since all assets are claimed by someone. A simplified balance sheet for a business making computer parts is shown in Figure 3-5.

The balance sheet is important because it reveals three key things about a business:

1. The ability of the business to pay its bills
2. The sources of capital in the business and how it is invested
3. The basis for measuring the earning power of the business on invested capital and total assets

MouseWorks' balance sheet shows that it has $51,000 in cash and $258,000 in total **current assets**. Current assets are expected to become cash within one year or less and are listed by their nearness to cash, or **liquidity**. **Accounts receivable** are bills sent to customers, which will become cash as soon as they are paid. **Inventories** are computer parts that MouseWorks is holding for resale to customers. They will become cash after they are ordered by customers, shipped and invoiced. **Prepayments** are items such as an insurance premium or rent that has been paid to others for future services to be rendered within the year. They represent a savings of cash because they reduce the future demand for cash on the business.

Figure 3-5   Mouseworks, Inc.
Balance Sheet
At: 12/31/97

Assets

Current Assets:	
Cash	$ 51,000
Accounts Receivable	180,000
Inventories	21,000
Prepayments	6,000
Total Current Assets	258,000
Non-Current Assets:	
Property & Equipment, Net	162,000
Total Assets	$420,000

Liabilities & Owners' Equity

Current Liabilities:	
Accounts Payable	$ 51,000
Accrued Payroll	9,000
Total Current Liabilities	60,000
Long-Term Liabilities:	
Long-Term Debt	108,000
Total Liabilities	168,000
Owners' Equity	
Common Stock (1,000 @$30/Sh.)	30,000
Retained Earnings	222,000
Total Owners' Equity	252,000
Total Liabilities & Owners' Equity	$420,000

The balance sheet also shows that MouseWorks has $60,000 in total **current liabilities**. Current liabilities are expected to consume cash within one year or less. **Accounts payable** are bills owed to suppliers of materials or services. **Accrued payroll** is wages and salaries owed to employees for services rendered. By the way, "accrue" is an accounting term that means to come into being over time. It typically applies to accounts that are owed but unpaid at the date of the financial statements like wages or interest income on investments. The balance sheet reveals that MouseWorks' ratio of current assets to current liabilities is 4.3 (258,000/ 60,000 = 4.3), or 430%. This is a good indication that MouseWorks has the capacity to pay its bills. The difference between current assets and current liabilities of $198,000 (258,000 - 60,000 = 198,000) is called **working capital**.

MouseWorks' balance sheet also reveals that the money invested in the business on a long-term basis comes from three sources. The first is 1,000 shares of **common stock** sold at $30 each, or $30,000 (1,000 x 30 = 30,000). This was paid in by the investors in exchange for stock and represents the ownership of the business. It entitles the shareholders to a proportionate share of the profits, dividends and voting rights. The original price of $30 per share is historical and has not the slightest influence on the price at which MouseWorks' shares trade in the market today.

The second is **retained earnings** of $222,000, which represents all undistributed profits of the business since it was formed. Retained earnings can be very large in businesses that have operated profitably for many years. It is important to remember that retained earnings, like profits, do not necessarily consist of cash, as you will see later in this section.

The third is **long-term debt**, or borrowings, of $108,000, which is not scheduled to be repaid in the current year. Long-term debt issued to the public is called **bonds**. The financial effect on the business of long-term debt and bonds is similar. There are no rights of ownership in the business attached to debt or bonds except if the business fails to meet either its interest or principal payments. This condition is called a **default**. In default, the claims on assets of the lenders or bondholders have priority over the claims of the shareholders.

These three items make up the **capital structure** of the business. The ratio of debt to owners' equity is .43 (108,000/252,000 = .43), or 43%. This is a reasonable ratio for a parts-manufacturing business such as MouseWorks. Owners' equity is sometimes called either total book value or **net worth**.

In addition, you can see that MouseWorks has invested $162,000 in noncurrent assets called property and equipment net of **depreciation**. Depreciation is the systematic recognition of wear and tear and technical obsolescence to which buildings, machinery and tools are subject over their useful lives. It is an expense of doing business, but, importantly, does not reduce the cash of the business.

The profitability of a business is most meaningful when it is shown as a percentage of both owners' equity and total assets. These measures permit comparison on a common basis with the performance of previous years as well as the performance of other businesses in the same industry. In MouseWorks' case, the owners' equity is $252,000 and the total assets are $420,000.

The second of the three financial statements is the income statement, which shows a comparison of sales, or **revenue**, and **expenses**. The difference is called **net income** or loss. Other terms commonly used for net income are **profit** and **earnings**. A simplified income statement for MouseWorks is shown in Figure 3-6. The income statement is important because it shows three key things about a business:

1. Profitability or lack of it
2. Nature and size of expenses
3. The basis for making projections of revenue and net income growth based on year-to-year trends

Happily, MouseWorks produced a profit, or net income, of $12,000 for the year ending 12/31/97. Net income, like retained earnings, does not necessarily consist of cash, as you will see later in this section. Net income represents 7.1% (12,000/168,000 = .071) of revenue, which at first glance seems very good for a parts manufacturer. We also can calculate annual **earnings per share (EPS)** by dividing net income by the number of common shares issued. MouseWorks' 1997 EPS is $12 (12,000/1,000 = 12), which also seems favorable. However, profitability as a percentage of owners' equity is an unimpressive 4.8% (12,000/252,000 = .048). This is called **return on equity (ROE)**. MouseWorks looks even weaker when profitability is related to total assets. This is called **return on assets (ROA)** and amounts to a paltry 2.9% (12,000/420,000 = .029). As you can see, profitability is most meaningful when it is related to a base such as revenue, owners' equity or total assets. As you will discover in later chapters of this book, MouseWorks appears to be a poor performer based on our look at these three measures.

Figure 3-6   MouseWorks, Inc.
Income Statement
Y/E: 12/31/97

Revenue		$168,000
Less Expenses:		
Cost of Goods Sold	$84,000	
Wages & Salaries	33,000	
Interest	18,000	
Insurance	3,000	
Depreciation	18,000	
Total Expenses		156,000
Net Income		$ 12,000

MouseWorks' largest expense is **cost of goods sold**. This account contains all the costs that were included in the parts shipped to customers during the year. Other major expenses of doing business during 1997 were labor, interest on debt, insurance and depreciation. Depreciation is the only one of these expenses that did not consume cash.

Growth trends in revenue and net income can be extended another year by adding 1997 results to our data about MouseWorks. Despite its historical nature, trend analysis can be helpful in projecting trends into the future and making investment decisions.

The third and final financial statement of a business is the statement of cash flows. It was required by GAAP recently in response to a need for more detailed information about cash, the lifeblood of every business. A business that is profitable and has good future prospects can still run out of cash and become unable to pay its bills. This condition is called **insolvency** and has caused many a business to sell out or declare bankruptcy. The importance of cash-flow management to a business is enormous. A simplified statement of cash flows for MouseWorks is shown in Figure 3-7.

Figure 3-7

MouseWorks, Inc.
Statement of Cash Flows
Y/E: 12/31/97

Cash Flows from Operations		
Collections from Customers	$42,000	
Payments to Employees	(54,000)	
Payments to Vendors	(45,000)	
Payments for Insurance	(9,000)	
Payments for Interest	(18,000)	
Net Cash Used for Operations		$ (84,000)
Cash Flows from Investing		0
Net Cash Used for Investing		0
Cash Flows from Financing		
Payment of Long-Term Debt	$(12,000)	
Payment of Dividends	(9,000)	
Net Cash Used for Financing		(21,000)
NET CHANGE + OR (-) IN CASH		$(105,000)
CASH, DECEMBER 31, 1996		156,000
CASH, DECEMBER 31, 1997		$ 51,000

The statement of cash flows is the accounting bridge between MouseWorks' beginning and ending cash balance for the year. These balances can be found on two consecutive, annual balance sheets, but the factors that caused the cash to change are not as clear. The statement of cash flows is important because it shows two key things about a business:

1. The business activities that produced cash during the year and how much
2. The business activities that consumed cash during the year and how much

Business activities are divided into three categories within MouseWorks' statement of cash flows. The first is operations, which relates to the basic business of making and selling computer parts to customers. Operations consumed $84,000 in 1997. As you can see, MouseWorks' net income of $12,000, as reflected in the income statement, and its net operating cash flow can be vastly different.

Incidentally, the method used here to present cash flows from operations is called the direct method because the sources and uses of cash are shown explicitly. It is also acceptable to use the indirect method, which reconciles net income to net cash flow from operations by adding back noncash expenses like depreciation and showing the changes in other account balances that affect cash. I find the direct method more understandable as an investor. Regardless of the method used, GAAP requires the presentation of a reconciliation of net income and cash flows from operations.

The second category of business activity is investing, which relates to the purchase and sale of property and equipment as well as securities held as investments. Investing activities produced no change in MouseWorks' cash during 1997.

The final category is financing, which relates to borrowing or repaying debt, issuance of stock, and payment of **dividends**. Dividends are cash payments to shareholders as part of the reward for being investors in a business. MouseWorks' investing activities consumed $21,000 in 1997.

The overall picture we get of MouseWorks from the statement of cash flows is cause for concern. The business is consuming cash at a very high rate. This might mean that the collectibility of the largest current asset on the balance sheet at year-end, accounts receivable of $180,000, is doubtful. This could stem from selling to financially weak customers or from poor performance of MouseWorks' computer parts that motivated customers to withhold payment. In either case, further investigation is called for.

Thankfully, this completes our discussion of accounting! You now may remove your armbands and green eyeshade. I have kept it as painless as possible in trying to honor my pledge to you. If you feel another reading of this section would be helpful, I urge you to do so after taking a well-deserved break. A basic understanding of the financial statements of a business is an important addition to your financial IQ.

4

CRITICAL CONCEPTS

In this section, you will discover that some of the best and brightest from America's colleges and universities have busied themselves with mathematical models and erudite descriptions of how the economy and investing works. Your first clue will be the use of Greek letters to replace plain English names, which is always a tip-off that the Ph.D.'s have discovered a new field of study to embrace. These folks are called "quants" because of the quantitative skills they bring to the table; their field of expertise is called **econometrics**. Quants have been recruited in droves at enviable salaries by **Wall Street** investment firms. On a more serious note, there have been enormous academic contributions in the last 40 years to the previously arcane business of investing. Now that we have sliced and diced the numbers, we are ready to tackle some selected concepts that lie at the heart of investing.

RISK AND REWARD

The most basic concept in investing is the relationship between risk and reward. Risk is the probability that an expected investing outcome, or reward, will not be realized. Risk consists of all the hazards—visible or hidden—that increase this probability. Reward is the expected benefit to be gained from the investment.

Investing bears a striking similarity to other human endeavors that require trading off risk and reward. For instance, a professional golfer standing on the teeing ground of a long par-four hole may select any of the 14 clubs in the bag to drive the ball. After analyzing the situation and conferring with his or her trusted adviser, the caddie, the decision turns on the expected advantage gained from distance versus accuracy. On a recent, rainy Sunday afternoon, I reviewed the driving statistics compiled from January 1 to May 3, 1998 for the top 150 players on the Professional Golf Association (PGA) Tour's Web site. After placing in groups the top, middle and bottom 10 players in driving distance, I averaged each group's distances and accuracy percentages. The accuracy percentage is based on the number of fairways hit; the risk of missing is one minus the accuracy. These crudely developed statistics are plotted in Figure 4-1.

Figure 4-1

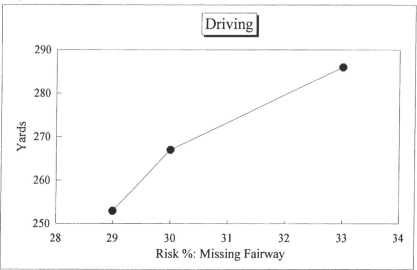

The relationship between the risk of missing the fairway and the driving distance is direct. For drivers in the bottom 253-yard group, the risk of missing was 29%; for drivers in the top 286-yard group, the risk of missing was 33%. Hey, if you are anything like me, you'd take the additional risk any day of the week just for the braggin' rights. And there you have just one of the many reasons you don't see me playing on the PGA Tour.

This points up the first axiom of investing. The more risk you assume, the greater the reward you should demand. This is how you get paid for taking risk. It is the reason a lender demands a higher interest rate on a loan from a new or marginally profitable business than the same lender demands from an established, highly profitable business. The lender judges that the new or marginally profitable business has less capacity to repay the interest and principal on time (risk) and charges a higher interest rate (reward) to compensate for this.

It also explains why you, as an American investor, would be inclined to pay more for a share of stock in an established American company with good prospects and an annual EPS of $1.00 than you would pay for a share of stock in a recently established company in the same business located in Brazil with the same prospects and annual EPS. From an operating point of view, the companies might be practically identical, but there are both visible and hidden hazards inherent in new enterprises, less-developed countries, and foreign-currency markets that enter into your determination of an acceptable price.

YIELD CURVE

The **yield** curve is a line that connects the yields on U.S. government debt securities with repayment, or **maturity**, dates ranging from less than 1 year to 30 years. Current yield is calculated by dividing a debt security's annual interest payments by the price for which it trades in the market. Because U.S. government debt securities are considered risk-free, the yield curve serves as a guide for all debts with similar maturities.

The yield curve is normally upward-sloping over time because investors are usually less certain about influences on future rates than rates closer to the present. In rare instances, the opposite sentiment prevails among investors and the resulting yield curve is downward-sloping, or **inverted**.

A typical yield curve is shown in Figure 4-2. Uncertainty about the future increases the farther out you look, so the shape of the yield curve makes intuitive sense based on our discussion of risk and reward.

Figure 4-2

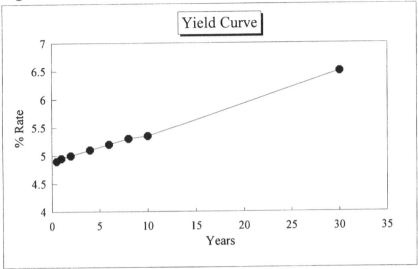

TIME HORIZON

Time horizon is the length of time you expect to remain invested before any withdrawals are needed. Americans are typically less patient and shorter term in their thinking than investors in other industrialized societies. These national character traits are often in direct conflict with success in investing because success in investing rarely is achieved in the short run without a great deal of either risk or luck. Patience in investing, on the other hand, is far more likely to produce good results year after year with less assumption of risk. This is particularly important to remember during a down market when there is a great deal of temptation to sell in response to bad news and declining prices. You must grit your teeth and hang on for the ride to resist this powerful temptation.

Patience and a long-term view are also important traits for investors when choosing the types of investments to own. An approximate ranking of the compound annual rates of return since 1926 for small and large common stocks, long-term government bonds, short-term treasury debt and inflation is shown in Table 4-1. In any given one- or two-year period, low-risk investments such as government bonds or short-term treasury debt might outperform the stock market in general and many individual stocks as well. However, in any given 20-year period since 1926, the U.S stock market has outperformed consistently—and often dramatically—all other financial assets. It never has lost money in any 20-year period since 1926. It also never has lost money in any 15-year period since 1941.

Table 4-1	Rank of Compound Annual Rates of Return 1926-1997 (Rounded)	
Small U.S. stocks		13%
Large U.S. stocks		11%
Long-term government bonds		5%
Short-term treasury debt		4%
Inflation		3%

Used with permission. ©1998 Ibbotson Associates, Inc. All rights reserved. [Certain portions of this work were derived from copyrighted works of Roger G. Ibbotson and Rex Sinquefield.]

This is called time diversification. It is based on the **law of large numbers**, or law of averages, which is the mathematical principle on which the insurance industry rests. Investment results cannot be predicted with certainty, but the more years you include, the more likely the good years will offset the bad, causing the collective results to resemble the average more closely. This is called **regressing to the mean**.

If you are seeking the highest available returns, you must be prepared to commit to stocks for upwards of 15 years despite their volatility. This takes discipline and, above all, an unswerving belief that patience will be rewarded. Several incidental benefits of long-term investing accrue to you as well. Individual holdings are less likely to be bought and sold, which results in less **turnover** in the portfolio. Lower turnover not only reduces brokerage fees, but also postpones the realization of capital gains and the related taxes in taxable portfolios. These factors will result in larger average investment returns measured in dollars after expenses and taxes. The reason for this is the simple fact that you have more money at work at any given time if fees are avoided and taxes are postponed. As you know, more investment dollars at work will produce more dollars of return, especially after compounding.

DIVERSIFICATION

Many of us grew up being regaled with the homespun logic of our elders who had lived through the **depression**. One such homily was "Don't put all your eggs in one basket!" This highlights the risk of nondiversification and makes a great deal of sense. You need only read the daily business press to see the enormous and frequent reversals that affect virtually all types of investments. In recent months, "Asian contagion" and imprudent trading in financial derivatives have been very much in the news. Excessive exposure to these risks has threatened the very survival of some companies, banks and municipalities. Additionally, some money managers have ended up with egg on their faces and clients heading for the exit. The lesson to be learned here is basic to sound long-term investing. It makes sense to spread your holdings both within and among asset classes. Asset classes include stocks, bonds and cash as well as a number of subcategories within these broad classes such as large, medium, small and foreign stocks. Think of your own experience. Precious few businesses depend on a single customer for all their orders. Similarly, very few businesses depend on a single product for all their sales. It is simply too risky to "put all your eggs in one basket."

Diversification can take many forms. You can diversify by types of investments, by individual companies, by industries and even by countries. You also can diversify by the **investment style** of the mutual-fund managers or investment advisers whom you hire. The probability that all elements of a well-diversified portfolio are highly correlated and will rise and fall in the same pattern at the same time is very low. This uncorrelated behavior will reduce the overall volatility, or risk, of the portfolio and likely produce better returns over the long term.

It is highly unlikely that you will select a handful of investments that consistently outperform the general market over the long term. Precious few professional investors—with the possible exception of the legendary Warren Buffett—ever do, so your chances are poor at best. Many investment professionals are convinced that the way in which you divide, or allocate, your holdings among asset classes is a far greater contributor to success than the individual stocks and debts you select. This approach is called **asset allocation** and is supported by a number of academic and empirical studies. Its proponents argue that because you cannot predict reliably the future direction of equity prices or interest rates, a portfolio that is diversified in the traditional sense—merely by sector of the economy and industry—is antiquated. You are better off to view your portfolio as a collection of buckets, the sizes of which are determined in part by your willingness to bear risk and in part by the total **market capitalization** of each of the major classes of assets. Into each bucket you then place either a focused mutual fund or a diversified sampling of individual securities that represents that bucket's asset class.

Asset allocation is akin to the manner in which a baseball manager arrays his or her fielders on the diamond. Since most balls are hit to the infield, there are more fielders there, but they are regularly spaced to eliminate large gaps through which to hit. No managers are ever certain where and when the opposition will hit the ball, so they cover all the bases to maximize the probability of the opposing hitter making an out. Similarly, the proponents of asset allocation acknowledge the impossibility of reliably predicting which asset classes will perform best and when, so they cover all the bases subject to their risk tolerances in rough proportion to market capitalization. In other words "being in all of the places, all of the time" is the name of the game.

EFFICIENT FRONTIER

In the last 40 years, a lot of academic brainpower has been focused on the risk and return characteristics of financial markets. The body of knowledge that has resulted is called **modern portfolio theory (MPT)** and won its developers the Nobel Prize in Economics. That alone should suggest that few of us will understand it fully, but let's take a look at some key points.

One of the seminal concepts in MPT is called the efficient frontier. It is a line that connects all the most favorable, or **optimum**, portfolios across all levels of risk. The asset mix, risk and average return of a representative portfolio starting with 100% bonds and ending with 100% stocks is tabulated in Table 4-2. As you can see, the lowest-risk portfolio consists of 25% stocks and 75% bonds. It has a variability of 11.25% and an average annual return of 10.2%. The efficient-frontier curve reflecting these data appears in Figure 4-3.

Table 4-2   Efficient Frontier
                           Risk vs. Reward

% Stocks	% Bonds	Average Risk %	Average Return %
0	100	12	9.5
10	90	11.5	9.8
25	75	11.25	10.2
50	50	12.25	10.9
75	25	14.4	11.6
90	10	16.1	12
100	0	17.4	12.4

The optimum portfolio—the one with the lowest risk and highest return—is the upper leftmost. I call this "goin' to Seattle." Imagine an outline of the Lower 48 laid over this chart. The upper-left corner, where Seattle is located, would represent a utopian portfolio of minimum risk and maximum return. By now, we all know we can't expect to "go to Seattle" because of the immutable link between risk and reward. Somehow I doubt that the developers of MPT ever talked in terms of "goin' to Seattle," but it sure helps me to think of the image in Figure 4-4. Another important feature of this chart is the lowering of risk achieved by mixing bonds with riskier stocks. This illustrates the effect that asset classes that are not highly correlated can have on risk.

Figure 4-3

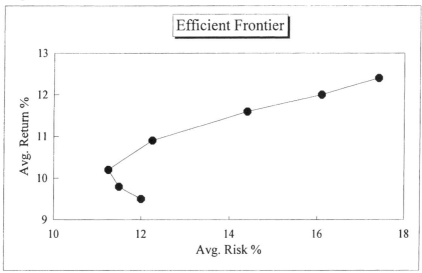

Figure 4-4

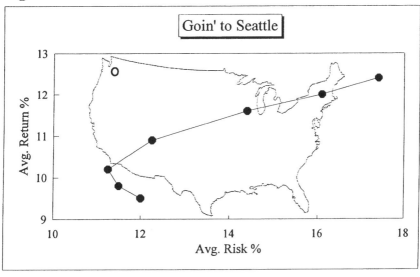

Some of you may find efficient-frontier charts hard to relate to because you have difficulty differentiating between the assumption of risk at the 11.25% and 17.4% levels. They may not seem far enough apart to justify leaving the additional average return on the table each year. You are not alone in that view. Many investors quip that "you can't take risk-adjusted returns to the bank," so why give up the additional return? This serves to highlight the fact that risk assumption is highly personal; each of us has to assess where our comfort zone lies on the efficient frontier.

OPPORTUNITY COST

If you decide to downshift your career and teach high-school algebra instead of remaining the highly compensated chief financial officer of DraconianWorks, you have sacrificed a certain amount of lifetime income. This amount is the opportunity cost of the decision to become a teacher.

The concept of opportunity cost applies equally to investing. If you place $10,000 in a bank passbook-savings account that pays 3% annual interest, you have sacrificed the interest you could have earned in a higher-yielding, insured money-market account. This amount can be measured precisely in dollars and is the opportunity cost of making the decision. For example, if the money-market account yields 5% annual interest, you have sacrificed $500 (10,000 X .05 = 500) per year. Whenever you choose among investment alternatives that require the same amounts of time and money, opportunity cost is present. It represents the economic value of what you sacrifice by making a choice.

SUPPLY AND DEMAND

The invisible mechanism by which securities are priced is called the law of supply and demand. It is a reflection of the collective behavior of the numerous buyers and sellers who populate the marketplace. It supposes that markets are unregulated and that we act rationally and in our own economic self-interest. Stocks and bonds are bought and sold on exchanges that are similar to an auction. Electronic and verbal, or **open outcry**, orders to buy and sell are received continuously from brokers all over the world. The exchange matches up orders in quantity and price and executes them for a fee.

If orders from buyers (demand) exceed orders from sellers (supply), competing buyers bid up the price to coax additional sellers to part with their securities. This causes prices to rise until demand is met or withdrawn. If orders from sellers (supply) exceed orders from buyers (demand), competing sellers lower the price to coax additional buyers to purchase. This causes prices to fall until supply is absorbed or withdrawn.

Prices in competitive securities markets are in constant flux as buyers and sellers are free to reappraise continuously the prospects and value of businesses in light of new information, economic events and, yes, even their own emotions, as you will see shortly.

HUMAN FRAILTY

You probably are thinking that this poor accountant has lost his balance. Why has he included a section on touchy-feely stuff like this? The answer lies in an emerging and important recognition by economists that many of us do not conform to the traditional model of rational behavior when it comes to money. You already knew this about love, pets and driving on the expressway, but money! Is nothing sacred? The following recognizable behavior patterns really impede our ability to maximize investment results:

1. *We hate to lose.* We Americans feel the regret of loss more acutely than the pleasure of gain. This leads us to be more risk-averse than investors should be. Some of us just can't stand seeing our stocks drop or admitting to friends we are temporarily in a loss position.

2. *We lack self-control.* This is hardly startling news to diet doctors, bartenders and credit counselors, but now economists have begun to see the light. We know we don't save enough. Perhaps to compensate, we also are attracted to investment vehicles that restrict access to (or impose withdrawal penalties on) our money to place it out of reach. These include annuities, whole life insurance and "Christmas club" savings plans, to name a few.

3. *We revise history.* We tend to recall selectively or minimize our poor investment decisions and dwell on the successes. This prevents us from learning fully from our mistakes and avoiding the same pitfalls again. We know from experience that stock tips rarely pan out, but we tend to remember the few that worked out and continue to act on them.

4. *We fail to see the big picture.* Economically, all money is the same, or **fungible**, yet we divide our money into mental accounts that have different characteristics. We know a home-equity loan is cheaper and tax-smarter than credit-card debt, yet we persist in running up the card balance. After all, we rationalize, the equity in our home is off-limits. Similarly, we are pleased as punch to spend our dividend checks, but balk at the idea of dipping into or borrowing against stock-market gains for a needed expenditure.

5. *We find comfort in crowds.* Most of us seek reaffirmation in our decisions and endeavors by following the crowd of our friends and associates. Speculative fever, which motivates us to purchase assets just because everyone around us is doing it, has led to many a loss. This kind of mania can cause us to buy at the top of the market in the hope that we will find a greater fool to whom we can sell at a profit. Quite often there is no greater fool to be found.

5

DEBTS

In this chapter, we will cover debts, the first of two broad classes into which all investments fall. The primary motivations to own them are interest-income production and preservation of capital. Debts include any contractual arrangement in which you lend money to a borrower for a specified period of time in exchange for two things:

1. Payment of interest at agreed upon times
2. Repayment of the loan amount, or **principal**

That's all there is to it! Debts are just that simple. However, like most simple things, debts come in a multiplicity of forms. Let's discuss the most common forms of debts and their features.

CASH

Savings accounts, money-market accounts, certificates of deposit due within a year and U.S. Treasury bills (T-bills) are all equivalent to cash from an investing point of view. Cash has negligible **default risk** and earns interest at a rate that is very close to the prevailing inflation rate. Unless cash is invested in tax-exempt securities, its interest income is taxable. Since you are taking almost no risk, you are rewarded accordingly with a very small or negative return after the current inflation rate and income taxes are subtracted away. This return, as you know, is called the after-tax real return.

Cash is generally considered a poor investment over a longer time horizon. It appears from time to time in investment portfolios as a result of recent sales of other holdings awaiting reinvestment as well as a safe harbor in times of great uncertainty. Additionally, individual investors often are advised to maintain a part of their portfolios in cash, perhaps, three to six months' living expenses, to guard against emergencies such as major, unplanned expenditures or job loss. While this is a cautious approach, holding cash is almost certain to result in underperforming other debt securities over a period of several years or more.

CERTIFICATES OF DEPOSIT

Certificates of deposit (CDs) are issued by banks and other chartered lending institutions. They typically range up to ten years in length, or maturity, and pay taxable interest at a fixed or adjustable rate. In the case of banks, the Federal Deposit Insurance Corporation (FDIC) guarantees up to $100,000 for each separately titled account, which eliminates the risk of principal and interest repayment. This is an extremely important safety feature of CDs. CDs are also easy to understand and locally available for most investors.

Because of their low risk, CDs are only marginally superior to cash in after-tax real return. Further, they often impose early withdrawal penalties and are not readily salable, or liquid. Finally, CDs can lock in your interest rate at a time of unforeseen inflation increases, which erodes your purchasing power.

FIXED-RATE ANNUITIES

Like a CD, a fixed-rate annuity is a contractual agreement between you and the issuer, an insurance company in this case. In exchange for the use of your money, the issuer promises a fixed interest rate for a set period—usually up to five years. At expiration, you have four options:

1. Withdraw all or part of your money
2. Contract with a new annuity issuer

3. Stay put, or **roll over**, with the existing issuer

4. Request **annuitization** after age 59 1/2

Unlike a CD, a fixed-rate annuity offers you tax-deferred compounding of your money. This tax-deferral feature is unique to the insurance industry and attests to the competitive advantages an industry can enjoy through favorable tax legislation. Tax-deferral lasts only until you withdraw money from your contract. The original investment, or principal, is always deemed to be withdrawn last, so the interest is immediately and fully taxable when withdrawn. Additionally, issuers may penalize early withdrawals with fees, which typically decline over time and are waived in certain hardship cases. Also, until age 59 1/2, the Internal Revenue Service (IRS) may impose a separate tax penalty for early withdrawal.

Table 5-1 shows an original investment of $10,000 earning 8% interest on both a taxable and tax-deferred basis. It assumes you are in the 31% income-tax bracket and shows the advantage in your account's value after 5 and 25 years. As you can see, tax-deferred compounding becomes powerful as the years increase. After 25 years, the advantage exceeds 30%, which is the crux of why tax deferral is such an attractive feature.

Table 5-1   Advantage of
                              Tax Deferral

Years Invested	$ Value of Taxable Account	$ Value of Tax-deferred Account	% Advantage
5	13,082	13,238	1.2
25	38,315	50,355	31.4

Insurance companies are subject to examination by state regulators and have a nearly spotless track record in honoring payments. This makes them very safe investments. Additionally, they are rated by a number of independent companies, the best known of which is A.M. Best. The Best's rating scale of financially secure insurers ranges from a high of A++ to a low of B+. A rating less than B+ is considered financially vulnerable and should be viewed with a jaundiced eye. The issuer's rating should always be reviewed prior to purchasing or rolling over an annuity.

Although most annuity purchasers leave them to their heirs, after age 59 1/2 you may unamendably elect to receive monthly payments for a period of at least five years to life. This unamendable election is called annuitization and has a unique tax advantage. The tax advantage lies in the calculation of the **exclusion ratio**, which governs how much of the monthly payment is a return of principal and, therefore, tax-free. The longer the payments last, the lower the exclusion ratio, until all the principal is returned. Notice that if you elect lifetime payments, this investment never quits paying you. This insurance feature appeals to retirees because it guarantees you won't run out of money before you depart this world. The downside to annuitization is that the interest rate may drop or be subject to an adjustment that makes it uncompetitive. Also, if you elect life income and expire shortly thereafter, you leave the entire account balance on the table. Even your heirs get nothing.

As you can see, fixed-rate annuities are hardly plain-vanilla investments. Because of their bells and whistles, I urge you to sit down with a competent and impartial adviser and walk through all the possible investment outcomes before you sign on the dotted line. Nonetheless, fixed-rate annuities have tax advantages, safety of principal, and contractual interest rates that are competitive with CDs. They are not salable, or liquid, and you take a beating in penalties if you change your mind before age 59 1/2. Finally, their after-tax real rate of return is better than other low-risk investments due in large part to the tax treatment they enjoy.

LIFE INSURANCE

Traditional life insurance is not really an investment. It is an income-replacement device that shifts the financial risk of premature death to the insurer. It consists of a contract, or **policy**, between the insurer and the **policyholder** that guarantees a stated death benefit will be paid to the **beneficiary** in exchange for a payment, or **premium**.

Life insurance comes in two basic forms. The first and simplest is term insurance. With term insurance, the entire premium is applied to the risk of the insured's death according to **mortality tables**. These tables are based on statistical life expectancies. Incidentally, the first true mortality table was created in 1693 by Edmond Halley, the British astronomer, who discovered the eponymous comet that appears every 76 years. The insurer can tolerate the collective risk of mortality because of the law of large numbers, which we discussed earlier in this book. Naturally, the premium rises as you age and approach relocation to the great beyond.

The second basic form of life insurance is permanent, or cash-value. With cash-value insurance you pay a higher, fixed premium that consists of the mortality portion described above and an excess that belongs to you, the policyholder. This excess is like a forced savings account that is invested at a nonnegotiable rate declared by the insurance company. The excess compounds tax-deferred, which is another nifty feature that only life insurers can offer. During your life, some or all of this excess and its tax-deferred earnings can be borrowed from the policy at a low rate of interest. Also, you can cash in, or **surrender**, the policy and receive your cash value back. Both these options may trigger income taxes.

If you genuinely need the income-replacement protection provided by life insurance, it can make sense to purchase it. This need is most likely to arise during the middle years of your life when you have dependents counting on your future earnings. At the younger and older ends of the age range, life-insurance needs are much less likely. However, the tax-free payment to your beneficiary could be a welcome source from which to pay estate taxes.

Life insurers are inventive marketers and are not about to let the securities industry eat their lunch without a fight. To remain competitive, they have concocted a wide and dazzlingly complex range of financial products from the two basic forms of insurance. Before purchasing any of these products, I urge you to sit down with a competent and impartial adviser and kill yourself on paper. I realize this sounds pretty grim and in poor taste, but it is the only way you will stand a ghost of a chance of grasping all the nuances of today's life-insurance products and making an informed comparison. As with fixed-rate annuities, I also urge you to review the rating of the insurer before purchasing any life-insurance product. Life insurance can have a place in your portfolio, but it is more of a risk-transfer device than a pure investment. It makes little sense to own if you do not need the income-replacement protection. It can be complex, expensive in the early years of ownership due to fees and commissions, and unlikely to perform as well as other asset classes over the longer haul.

U.S. TREASURY BONDS

U.S. Treasury bonds (T-bonds) are debt securities auctioned by the U.S. Treasury to finance the federal budget. Shorter-maturity debt securities are called T-notes. They are backed by the full faith and credit of the U.S. government and are considered risk-free for that reason. When originally issued, T-notes range from 2 to 10 years in maturity and T-bonds range from 10 to 30 years in maturity. After issuance, they are traded actively on exchanges and can be purchased with almost any remaining maturity you like. They are then called **seasoned**. They pay interest every six months, which is subject to federal income tax only. Thirty-year T-bonds usually pay the highest risk-free rate available in the market, as you would expect from your understanding of the yield curve. The interest rate is expressed as an annual percent of the principal, or **face amount**, of the bonds, which is typically $1,000. This is called the **nominal rate**, or **coupon**, and rarely reflects the effective rate, or yield, because as the bonds freely trade in the market, the price is reset continuously by supply and demand. The face amount is repaid at maturity.

It is crucial for you to understand that the price, or market value, of an existing bond moves in the opposite direction of prevailing market interest rates. This is called an inverse relationship. In other words, if an existing 30-year T-bond with 20 years remaining to maturity that has a coupon of 7.5% trades in the market while prevailing 20-year rates are also 7.5%, it will attract buyers at the face amount of $1,000. This is because buyers are unable to find alternative bonds with similar characteristics at a lower price.

However, if the prevailing 20-year rate rises to, say, 9%, new 20-year issues coming to market will necessarily yield 9% in order to attract buyers. This means that an existing 7.5% bond will decline in price to the amount that makes a coupon of 7.5% yield the 9% available on the newly issued bond. This sounds complicated, but the amount can be found readily using **yield-to-maturity** tables. Under these conditions, the 7.5% bond is now worth $863 because this is the price at which the bond will attract buyers. This decrease of $137 below the face amount is called a **discount**. Conversely, if the prevailing 20-year rate declines to, say, 6%, new 20-year issues coming to market will necessarily yield 6% because it is sufficient to attract buyers. This means that an existing 7.5% bond will rise in price to the amount that makes a coupon of 7.5% yield 6%. Again, using yield-to-maturity tables, you can find readily that the 7.5% bond is now worth $1,172. This increase of $172 above the face amount is called a **premium**.

By the time the bond matures, the discount or premium will disappear because the bondholder is entitled to receive only the face amount of $1,000. This process of disappearing over time is called **amortization**. It affects the yield-to-maturity calculation, but is, thankfully, figured in the tables. I know this is giving you a headache to read. I'm getting one just writing it, but this is worth repeating. *Bond prices move inversely to yield!* Therefore, bonds, especially longer-term issues, can be very volatile, or risky, despite their image as conservative, grandfatherly investments. Not surprisingly, this risk is called **interest-rate risk**. While you may accuse me of being a frustrated word carpenter, I have found that acronyms help me remember things. Because I attach such importance to the price-yield relationship of bonds, I offer you **PITY**: Price Inverse To Yield. If you forget everything else in this chapter, remember PITY! Treasury notes and bonds can be safe, risk-free producers of taxable income if they are held to maturity. If they are sold prematurely, the interest-rate risk can result in price gains or losses. The latter might be a real pity!

MUNICIPAL BONDS

Municipal bonds (Munis) are fixed-income securities issued by states, counties and municipalities for public projects for which they currently cannot pay, such as toll roads, airports and libraries. They come in various maturities and pay either tax-exempt, double tax-exempt or triple tax-exempt interest every six months. The latter two only apply if you, the investor, reside in the state of the issuer. Despite the tax-exempt status of their interest income, capital gains and losses in Munis are treated just the same as their taxable counterparts. Munis are traded actively in the market, which makes them liquid.

Munis fall into two categories called revenue bonds (Revenues) and general obligation bonds (GOs). The security of Revenues is tied to the cash flow of a specific project such as a toll road. If motorists choose to avoid the toll and use alternate roadways, the Revenues issued to finance the road might not be repaid. This is called default risk. The security of GOs is backed by the full faith and credit of the issuer. Like T-bonds, this means that all general tax and fee revenue of the issuing entity is available for repayment of the bonds. This greatly reduces default risk. Private repayment insurance is often attached to both types of Muni issuances, which shifts the risk of default from you to the insurer. As you would expect, the cost of this insurance reduces slightly the yield of the insured Munis, but is a small price to pay for the peace of mind it brings.

A troublesome feature of many Munis is the issuer's contractual right to repay, or **call** away, the bonds at stated intervals prior to their natural maturity. Issuers prefer **callable** bonds because they can refinance more cheaply if rates fall. This **call feature** really can rain on your parade if rates fall sharply. You will be forced to reinvest more money than you receive to replace the yield you give up. As you know, that is because bond prices move in opposition to yield.

If your income-tax bracket is 28%, Munis are somewhat attractive because their yield usually tends to fall between 70% and 85% of the yield of a comparable T-bond. Therefore, Munis put slightly more money in your pocket after taxes. If your federal income-tax bracket is even higher, say, 31%, 36% or 39.6%, Munis are that much more rewarding after taxes. Conversely, if you are in the lowest federal income-tax bracket of 15%, Munis don't work for you.

The Muni yield that is directly comparable to a taxable bond is called the **tax-equivalent yield**. It is computed by subtracting your decimal income-tax rate from one and dividing the result into the Muni yield. For example, if your income-tax rate is 31%, or .31, the tax-equivalent yield of a Muni with a 4.85% yield would be 7.03% (4.85/(1.00 - .31) = 7.03). If the comparable T-bond yield stood at 6.33%, you would pick up .7% (7.03 - 6.33 = .70) additional yield annually. Incidentally, in bond-investing jargon, .7% is called 70 **basis points** to avoid confusion in working with such small quantities. Every 1% consists of 100 basis points.

A complete tax-equivalency chart reflecting the above example is shown in Table 5-2. This chart makes it easy to see that the wisdom of owning Munis instead of comparable taxable bonds is driven by your tax bracket. Despite the call risk, Munis can be safe, low-risk producers of tax-exempt income if they are held to maturity. If they are sold prematurely, you are faced with the same interest-rate risk that all bonds present.

Table 5-2 Tax-equivalent Yield %
Muni versus T-bond

Investor Tax Bracket	Muni Yield	Tax-equivalent Muni Yield	Comparable T-bond Yield	Muni Better (Worse) Basis Pts.
15%	4.85	5.71	6.33	(62)
28%	4.85	6.74	6.33	41
31%	4.85	7.03	6.33	70
36%	4.85	7.58	6.33	125
39.6%	4.85	8.03	6.33	170

MORTGAGES

Mortgages are long-term loans taken out by borrowers to purchase homes. They typically have maturities ranging up to 30 years and either floating or fixed interest rates. They are secured by the value of the home, which can be sold to satisfy the debt if the borrower defaults. Believe it or not, you can invest in screened pools of other people's mortgages and indirectly collect their monthly payments! Mortgages have very low default risk and are traded actively in the market. They also pay monthly and yield more than comparable T-bonds. There are several distinct investment vehicles that are based on mortgages. These include the securities of the Government National Mortgage Association (GNMA), the Federal National Mortgage Association (FNMA) and collateralized mortgage obligations (CMOs). Our discussion will be general and thus will cover them all.

Mortgages have two features that make them unique. The first is that most mortgages require payment against, or amortization of, principal in every monthly payment. Since the payments are all equal, the principal component is smaller in the early years and larger as maturity nears. This means that your monthly check is fully taxable to the extent interest is received. The principal represents a return of your investment and is not taxable. If you wish to keep the same amount of money invested in mortgages, you must reinvest these returns of principal periodically to stay even. The second unique feature is the contractual right of the borrower to prepay the mortgage. This occurs when a borrower sells the home or refinances to take advantage of lower prevailing rates. It has much the same effect as the call feature in Munis and presents you with the same **reinvestment risk**. Sales occur somewhat randomly, but refinancings almost always punish your yield because rates have fallen when the principal is returned to you. Because of these features, mortgages are slightly riskier than T-bonds, but reward you with greater income production. Mortgages offer less potential for gain than other types of bonds because the borrower can—and probably will—prepay as soon as rates drop sharply.

CORPORATE BONDS

Corporate bonds (Corporates) are the long-term public debts of private corporations. Corporations issue debt to raise capital for uses like repaying, or **retiring**, other higher-cost debt, plant modernization and acquiring other businesses for cash. Corporations sometimes prefer issuing debt instead of stock because the interest on debt that they pay is a corporate tax deduction. They also may prefer debt because stock issuance reduces, or **dilutes**, the EPS of the business, causes cash-dividend payments to increase and creates additional voting rights. Whenever debt is added to the balance sheet of a business, leverage is increased.

Corporates are secured by a priority claim over owners on the assets of the business and usually pay fixed interest every six months. Like Munis, some Corporates contain call features. Unlike T-bonds, insured Munis and mortgages, Corporates require continuous attention to the risk that the issuer will default on either the interest or principal payments called for in the bond contract, or **indenture**. This is called **credit risk**. Several well-established and independent companies, including Moody's and Standard & Poor's (S&P), provide ratings for practically all major Corporates, which are regularly updated. These ratings are very rigorous and permit investors to assess credit quality before and during ownership of fixed-income securities. S&P ratings range from a high of triple A (AAA) to a low of single D (D), which indicates default. Corporates above BB are considered **investment grade** by institutional investors. By the way, Munis are rated in much the same way. Muni ratings should be monitored also, especially if your bonds are not insured.

In today's world of corporate **mergers, acquisitions, spin-offs**, and **recapitalizations**, it is essential to monitor continuously the ratings of corporate securities because the issuer's financial condition literally can change for better or worse overnight. As you would expect from your knowledge of risk and reward, credit quality is inverse to yield for Corporates with the same maturity. AAA-rated Corporates would yield the least; BB- or lower-rated Corporates would yield the most. Rational investors demand more yield for assuming more risk, wouldn't you? This relationship is shown in Figure 5-1.

Figure 5-1

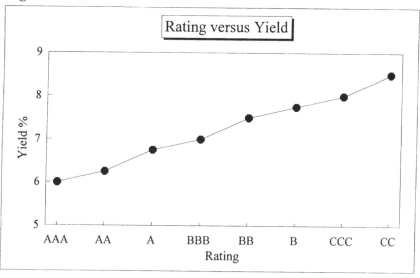

Not surprisingly, the shape of this line is strikingly similar to the T-bond yield curve. Yield rises in response to credit risk just as it typically does in response to uncertainty about future interest rates. Corporates rated BB or lower are called **high-yield bonds**. Many bonds at the lower end of the high-yield rating spectrum are **junk bonds**. This is one of the few investing terms that requires no further explanation! Junk bonds are a more recent creation of Wall Street **investment bankers** and are issued by companies for corporate takeovers of other businesses instead of issuing more stock or paying from existing cash. Incidentally, the architect of junk bonds served a prison sentence as his reward for designing them. Many federally guaranteed savings and loan associations (S&Ls) bought them in the 1980s as high-yield investments and received a harsh lesson in credit risk when the prices of their holdings dropped like a stone. Some of the executives and directors of these banks are probably still looking for work today. In default, junk bondholders are among the last entitled to assert their claim on the issuer's assets. This condition is described as **subordinated**, or **junior**, and can mean that you recover very little—or none—of your accumulated interest and principal after the **senior** creditors are satisfied.

Corporates range from low-risk, steady producers of fully taxable interest income to high-yield and junk bonds that pay you more interest for assuming more risk. They are subject to all the same risks as other debt securities as well as credit risk. Corporates are a good choice for income-oriented investors seeking maximum taxable yield. The key is finding the blend of risk and yield that is comfortable for you.

ASSET-BACKED DEBTS

Asset-backed securities (ABSs) vividly demonstrate the creative imagination of today's Wall Street investment-banking community. This class of debts is backed by pools of future cash receipts due the issuer. They permit the issuer, usually a bank or financial-services company, to convert to immediate cash assets on their books such as credit-card accounts, car loans and home-equity loans. These assets serve as backing, or **security**, for the issuance and are more risky than the issuer's own promise to repay. For that reason, ABSs carry a higher yield that contains a **risk premium**.

ABSs behave much like short-term, junior corporate debts, but are not callable. Corporate ABSs are fully taxable and typically have maturities of five years or less. The leading credit agencies rate each issuance and this rating should be monitored closely. In some cases, the rating services require insurance in exchange for a good rating. Institutional investors such as pension funds and insurance companies are large purchasers of ABSs. They are attracted to the short maturity, which reduces price volatility, and the high yield.

ABSs have really pushed the creative envelope. Recently, ABSs have been issued that are backed by taxicab medallions, moneygrams to Mexico from immigrant workers, hair-transplant fees, student loans and security-alarm contracts. My personal favorite is a ten-year ABS issued in 1997 by David Bowie, the British rocker, which is secured by the future royalties on some of his former hits. It is reported that Prudential Insurance Company of America bought the entire issuance, which gives new meaning to "owning a piece of the rock." The investing landscape is certainly ch-ch-ch-changing!

You should be aware of ABSs as they become more widely accepted as short-term, high-yield securities. Credit insurance can make them safe and their yield is often very attractive compared to comparable government debts or CDs.

ZERO-COUPON BONDS

Zero-coupon bonds (Zeros) are among the most straightforward of fixed-rate investments. A government, corporate or municipal issuer borrows your money in exchange for a promise to repay a higher face amount at maturity. That's it! There is no interest payment or coupon. The yield is the compound rate that grows your principal from the **deep discount** price you pay the issuer to the face amount of the security at maturity. It comes right out of the future value formula we discussed earlier in this book.

Issuers like Zeros because all the demand on their cash is postponed to the maturity date. Under GAAP, they still must reflect the notional, or **accreted**, interest expense in their financial statements. Investors like Zeros because they will receive a known yield and face amount at maturity. Also, they are attracted to the absence of reinvestment risk since no cash payments are received until maturity. Finally, the high rate sensitivity of Zeros is attractive to some very aggressive investors because large price gains are possible if rates drop sharply. The legendary Warren Buffett recently gave the investing community a salutary lesson in this area with Zeros. If rates rise, investors can always hold the Zeros to maturity and suffer no loss. Corporate and municipal Zeros are subject to the same rate, call and credit risk as their interest-bearing counterparts. Constantly reviewing the credit ratings of your current or contemplated holdings is a must.

There are two unique disadvantages of Zeros. First, you receive no current cash since it is all applied to principal growth within the security. Secondly, the accreted interest from government and corporate Zeros is subject to federal tax each year even though you receive no cash from the security with which to pay the taxes. Additionally, the accreted interest from corporate and Muni Zeros is subject to state tax each year unless you reside in the Muni issuer's state. This is a real incentive for individual investors to avoid all but certain Muni Zeros. Zeros are also relatively expensive to buy and sell through brokers. Zeros are traded actively and, therefore, liquid, but really have no use as income-producing investments. They are best suited for a tax-deferred retirement account or a child's college fund where a set amount is certain to be paid at maturity.

TREASURY INFLATION-PROTECTION SECURITIES

Treasury inflation-protection securities (TIPS) are a recent experiment by the U.S. government to test the investor acceptance of inflation-indexed debt. At the moment, only 5- and 10-year maturities are available, but a 30-year bond is being rolled out in April 1998. TIPS are hybrid securities that contain an annual adjustment to the principal for inflation or deflation based on the consumer price index (CPI). Like Zeros, this adjustment is deemed accreted interest and is subject to federal income tax only. Additionally, a cash interest rate over and above the inflation adjustment is set by auction and paid on the adjusted principal amount every six months. This is also subject to federal income tax.

At first glance, this all seems attractive, but there are a few possible disadvantages. If the CPI rises sharply, you may receive less cash from TIPS than the tax due on the cash interest plus the accretion to principal, unless you own them in a tax-deferred account. This is more likely if your income-tax bracket is high, say, 36% or 39.6%. Second, the Department of Labor has tinkered from time to time with the way the CPI is calculated. This possibility has a chilling effect on investors in TIPS because the principal adjustments are CPI-driven. Third, like Zeros, some of the cash return is postponed to maturity. This renders TIPS unsuitable for income investors. Finally, the market for TIPS is undeveloped at this writing, so liquidity could be a problem if you must sell your TIPS prior to maturity. The advantages of TIPS are safety of principal, purchasing-power protection and lower volatility. They are unsatisfactory producers of current income, but have appeal if you seek diversification and are convinced it is more likely than not that inflation will rear its ugly head.

FOREIGN BONDS

The foregoing debts have all been U.S.-based and denominated in U.S. dollars. If you have an irrepressible yearning to visit distant and exotic places, foreign debts will take you there.

The basic issues confronting foreign debtholders are the same as in U.S. debts with three important exceptions. The first is cross-correlation. Since the economic and political influences on interest rates and investor sentiment can be vastly different from one country to the next, foreign government, or sovereign, debt and foreign corporate bonds may behave in a different pattern than similar U.S. securities. This lack of correlation can reduce portfolio volatility over time. When one is up, the other may be down, which offsets the range, or amplitude, of swings in portfolio return. Second, foreign issuers are subject to political risk, which largely is ignored by domestic U.S. investors in their own securities. Political risk can run the gamut from internal tax or fiscal policy changes all the way up to a declaration of war. History is replete with examples of political risk impacting the value of foreign assets. Third, unless the debt security is denominated in U.S. dollars—and many are—it is subject to currency risk. Currency risk has a direct and immediate effect on the price of a security. If you own British government bonds and the pound weakens 5% against the U.S dollar, your bonds and interest payments are now worth 5% less. If the British pound strengthens against the U.S. dollar, the inverse occurs. Remember, the local investors in Britain are not feeling your pain or joy for they continue to spend and measure results in pounds, not dollars. Although you may be told that currency risk is avoidable or insurable, it really is not at an economical cost. Further, one of the motives for owning foreign debt securities is the diversification they add to your portfolio, so why pay to eliminate this risk?

As a U.S. taxpayer, your global income is subject to tax. Foreign-source interest income and capital gains are treated just like their fully taxable U.S. counterparts with one notable exception. Nearly all foreign countries require tax on interest to be withheld prior to remitting the funds to foreign debtholders. Happily, most of these countries have tax treaties with the U.S. that entitle you to claim in your U.S. tax return either a full credit or itemized deduction for foreign taxes paid. In those cases where no such treaty exists, you are taxed twice. Our neighbors to the south, the Latin American countries, are the most notable examples of this tax treatment. Predictably, the yields on their debt instruments are marginally higher to compensate for this.

Foreign debt securities issued by stable nations and corporations can be strong income producers and portfolio-risk reducers at the same time. The debt instruments themselves contain the same risks as fully taxable U.S. debts. Additionally, currency and political risks are always present, so you should diversify among issuing nations and regions of the world to reduce these risks.

LOANS TO FRIENDS AND RELATIVES

I know you must think this poor accountant has taken leave of his senses yet again by including this nonsense in a serious book. The fact is, I get asked about this so often that I feel compelled to cover it with you. There are two—and only two—rules on making loans to friends and relatives. They are:

1. Only become a lender to friends and relatives if you can afford to lose four things. They are, in order of importance: your principal, your interest, your friendship, and your dignity.
2. Read rule number one again.

If the idea or need is genuine and the borrower has the capacity to repay you, send him or her to a bank. That's what they do all day long for a living. If that seems harsh and insensitive, I have a litany of sad tales about broken friendships, resentment and unhappiness stemming from these kind of loans to share with you. On a kinder and gentler note, if someone close to you needs money that badly, give it to them free and clear, if you simply must. They will try to repay you voluntarily, if they are worthy of your trust. If they do not even try to repay you, file the experience under "lessons in life" and move on. Incidentally, during your life you can give $10,000 per year, for as many years as you like, to just about any person on this planet free from gift tax. Beginning in 1999, this annual exclusion amount will be indexed for inflation.

SUMMARY OF DEBTS

This concludes our discussion of debts. As you now can see, they come in all sorts of forms with all sorts of features. The key is clearly defining what you want to accomplish financially by owning debts and which risks you are prepared to accept in exchange.

6

EQUITIES

In this chapter, we will cover equities, the second broad class into which all assets fall. The primary motivation for owning them is gains in price. Equities are rights of direct ownership in assets and proportionately entitle you to three basic things:

1. Ownership of profits and losses
2. Dividends, if any
3. Voting rights

Over time horizons of 15 years or more, equities have been the clear winner in the race for both absolute and risk-adjusted investment returns. Upon sale, price gains in equities held at least a year may be taxed at lower rates than interest or dividend income, which can provide an additional incentive to own them. In the event the issuer fails, holders of equity receive no payment in bankruptcy or **liquidation** unless and until all senior creditors are satisfied. In this case, the value of your securities becomes decorative and they can be used as kitty litter or as wallpaper for the basement workshop. The most common forms of equities and their features are discussed below.

COMMON STOCKS

Common stocks are direct ownership in one of the legal community's most brilliant creations, the corporation. A corporation is an entity that can conduct business, own assets, borrow money, and defend lawsuits without exposing its owners to personal financial risk beyond their investment. This business form has enormous advantages and continues to serve as a platform for entrepreneurial activity that otherwise would be far too risky to undertake personally.

Additionally, corporations can sell stock in affordable quantities to a large number of private or public buyers. This makes raising money much easier than finding a few investors with very deep pockets and the potential to gain control of the business through concentrated voting power. Stock issuance also gives a corporation succession of ownership that can last indefinitely. Businesses often elect to issue stock instead of borrowing money for several reasons. First, debt places an ongoing demand on cash for periodic interest payments called **fixed charges**, which raises the cost of doing business. Second, the financial risk of the business is increased through the use of leverage. In contrast, stock issuance places no demand on cash unless the board of directors of the business votes to **declare** a cash dividend. This decision can be made quarterly and no legal obligation requires it be maintained. Finally, stock issuance actually reduces the financial risk of the business by **deleveraging** its capital structure.

When common stock is first issued to the public by a previously private company, the process is called an **initial public offering (IPO)**. This requires the private owners to reduce their stake in the business and admit new owners. Once a business has sold shares to the public, it is called a **public company**. Public companies are eligible to be listed on an **exchange**, if they can meet its listing requirements, and are subject to SEC oversight. A public company has new and additional responsibilities, including publishing audited financial statements and reporting certain significant transactions such as sales and purchases of its own stock by directors and management. A public company can issue additional shares as often as the company **charter** permits, provided demand exists for the shares. This is called a **secondary offering**.

Increasing the number of shares of stock causes the same net profit of the business to be divided among a larger number of owners. Imagine buying a pie for six people and then learning at the last minute that your aunt Florence from South Bend and her two teenage sons, who play right and left defensive tackle for Notre Dame, are in town and coming for dinner. You must now cut the exact same pie into nine pieces, so everyone has an equal but smaller slice. This is called **dilution**. Secondary offerings usually occur when the price of already issued, or **outstanding**, shares is high to minimize the effect of dilution. Gauging demand, setting a price range, and facilitating, or **underwriting**, the issuance of the initial and any secondary share offerings has traditionally been the work of investment bankers who are hired for a fee by the issuer. Also, the SEC must approve every public offering of shares and carefully reviews the registration documents, or **prospectus**, in its role as protector of the investing public's interest.

Once the shares are issued, they are traded among buying and selling investors—both individual and **institutional**. The issuing business receives its cash, and the subsequent price of the shares in the **secondary market** is set by supply and demand. If this all sounds too good to be true, it is! The corporate form of ownership has a price. It is **double taxation**. The first layer of tax is imposed on corporate net income, or earnings. The second layer of tax is imposed on you, the equity holder, since distributions of corporate earnings as dividends are fully taxable at federal rates ranging up to 39.6% plus your state income-tax rate. This disadvantage can be minimized or avoided if you own stocks paying low or no dividends. In 1996, corporations paid $172 billion in federal income taxes. This was about 26% of the $656 billion in federal income taxes paid by individuals like you and me. Like interest on debts, the dividend income of a stock comprises its yield. The yield percentage is computed by dividing the annual dividend per share by the stock price. In the case of MouseWorks, the company we analyzed in the accounting section, $9,000 was paid as dividends in 1997. MouseWorks had 1,000 common shares, so the dividend per share was $9 (9,000/1,000 = 9). If MouseWorks' shares were trading at $132, the yield would be 6.8% (9/132 = .068). This yield is very high in comparison to the current overall market average of less than 2%. As we saw, MouseWorks' financial condition looked suspect, so the price of the shares may have fallen, driving up the yield. What a pity!

Common stock permits you to own a part of virtually any business you like. Common stock is usually classified by three attributes. The first is the total value of the outstanding shares, or market capitalization, of the issuer. This is called market cap for short and is shown in descending order in Table 6-1, which also shows the relevant market index. Each index represents all the stocks that fall into a size range and is the best indicator to use when judging investment performance against the market as a whole. As of October 1998, the stocks that alone made up the **Standard & Poor's (S&P) 500 index** accounted for about 70% of the value of all U.S. stocks. As stock prices rise, companies may migrate north to higher categories due to their increased market cap. Hopefully, you won't own many stocks that migrate south.

Table 6-1   Range of Market
Capitalization
($ Millions)

Name	$ Range	Relevant Market Index
Large-Cap	over 5,000	S&P 500
Mid-Cap	1,000 to 5,000	S&P 400
Small-Cap	100 to 999	Russell 2000
Micro-Cap	under 100	Russell 2000

The second attribute is the orientation, or **tilt**, of the stock. Generally, stocks are judged to be **growth** or **value** in orientation. Growth stocks have rapidly expanding earnings, pay no or low dividends, and are expensive, or at a **premium**, relative to the market index. Value stocks have slowly expanding or even cyclical earnings, pay higher, consistent dividends, and are cheap, or at a **discount**, relative to the market index. A premium or discount to the market is measured in terms of the **price/ earnings (P/E) ratio**. The P/E ratio also often is called the **earnings multiple**. The P/E ratio is computed by dividing the stock price by the annual earnings per share (EPS). For example, PachydermWorks, a large-cap growth stock trading at $50 per share with an EPS of $2, has a P/E ratio of 25 (50/2 = 25). If the S&P 500 index were trading at an earnings multiple of 22, PachydermWorks' shares would be at a premium to the market. Conversely, MouseWorks, a micro-cap value stock trading at $132 per share with an EPS of $12, has a P/E ratio of 11 (132/12 = 11). If the Russell 2000 index traded at an earnings multiple of 20, MouseWorks' shares would be at a deep discount to the market. As you saw in the section on accounting, this deep discount is justified.

Table 6-2   Stock Industry
                        Groups

Group	Subgroup
1. Basic Materials	Forest products
2. Independent	Plantations
3. Consumer, Cyclical	Home construction
4. Consumer, Non-cyclical	Medical supplies
5. Energy	Oil drilling
6. Financial	Regional banks
7. Industrial	Heavy machinery
8. Technology	Software
9. Utilities	Electricity

The third attribute is industry group. There are nine broad U.S. industry groups, which are listed in Table 6-2 with an example of each. These nine U.S. industry groups contain over one hundred subgroups. Virtually all of these subgroups contain large and small stocks as well as growth and value stocks. As you can plainly see, this abundance of choices has something for every investor.

Common stocks also can be fully taxable, but growing, dividend-income producers. This is especially true of utility stocks, which pay higher dividends because their price-appreciation potential is often limited due to government regulation of the rates they may charge customers. Dividend growth is an important element of value and can cushion the decline in price of a stock in down markets.

As with corporate debt, the financial condition of common-stock issuers should be analyzed carefully using an approach similar to the one we applied to MouseWorks in the section on accounting. As a cogent reminder, Montgomery Ward and Zenith Electronics, two of the companies I best remember from the days in which I was growing up near Chicago, are on life support. I still remember to this day Zenith's advertising slogan: "The quality goes in before the name goes on." The grim reaper of corporate failure never sleeps! Despite the inherent risks, owning common shares in good businesses has made more money for long-term investors than any other single asset class. Upon sale, common stocks are also tax-friendly because you can decide when to sell them and you may pay taxes at the lower capital-gains rate.

PREFERRED STOCKS

These hybrid securities are neither fish nor fowl because they combine features of debts and equities in one security. They were named not because investors prefer them, but rather due to their legal standing in dividend entitlement and default. Preferred stockholders get first bite at the apple when earnings are distributed as dividends. Preferred stock typically carries a high, fixed dividend rate based on its face value. Unless and until the preferred dividend is satisfied, no dividends can be paid to the common shareholders. Similarly, in liquidation, preferred stockholders share in any remaining assets of the issuer after lenders, but before common shareholders.

Preferred stock often has no vote in the affairs of the company unless previously declared dividends are owed to preferred shareholders. This condition is called an **arrearage**. Also, preferred stock is frequently **callable** for cash at a small premium over face value. As a result, preferred stock can be a low-volatility, steady producer of income, but it lacks the potential for both dividend increases and large capital gains that is available to owners of common stock in the same company unless it is **convertible**. Convertible preferred stock contains a feature that permits the owner to exchange preferred shares for common shares at a stated ratio. If the common shares appreciate to a level that makes conversion attractive, you can have your cake and eat it too. You receive a high dividend yield as well as potential for capital gain. Convertible preferred is often issued by companies that seek to entice investors with its bells and whistles because their track record is spotty, so watch out! You must perform your credit-risk homework with these securities diligently. Because convertible preferred stock is issued infrequently, the market is limited, or **thin**, which can make selling difficult.

Although hardly plain-vanilla, preferred stocks are candidates for conservative, diversified portfolios if you clearly understand their features and terms. However, the same investment objectives often can be met in a more easily understandable manner with a combination of debt securities and common stock.

FOREIGN STOCKS

Like their U.S. counterparts, foreign, or international, companies issue stock to raise capital. The mechanics of issuance and the features of the shares are much the same as with U.S. common stock. Additionally, the tax issues with respect to cash dividends and capital gains are the same as those discussed in the section on foreign debts. Most foreign stocks are issued and traded on exchanges within the country where the issuer's headquarters is located, or domiciled. These are called **local exchanges**. Naturally, the stock prices and cash dividends, if any, are denominated in local currency.

Despite their size and familiarity, U.S. stock markets represent just 50% of the approximately $12.5 trillion in global equities based on market caps at 12/31/97. This means that you must venture outside U.S. borders to participate in the many excellent foreign companies that make up the other 50%. After the U.S., the three largest stock markets in descending order are Japan, the United Kingdom and Germany; they had a combined market cap of about $3.4 trillion at 12/31/97. Currently, there are functioning stock markets in some 46—and still counting—foreign nations. These countries are home to some of the largest companies in the world in their respective industries. Names like Mitsubishi, Nestle, Nokia and Polygram can compete with the best of companies in their global importance. Smaller markets like Peru, Thailand and Zimbabwe are called **emerging** because their capital markets are in their infancy. Foreign stocks differ from their U.S. counterparts in the same three characteristics discussed in the section on foreign debts, namely, lack of correlation to U.S. securities, political risk, and currency risk. Additionally, stocks traded in small, emerging markets can be illiquid, especially in down markets, when everyone heads for the exit at the same time.

Despite its recent surge, the U.S. market index only rarely ranks number one in the world. For example, in 1997, the U.S. market recorded yet another handsome return of 34.1%, but ranked tenth in the world without regard to market cap. The top ten performers in descending order along with their market caps in U.S. $ billions are set forth in Table 6-3. At the same time, the worst-performing markets in the world were also foreign. Asia alone had five nations whose stock markets in 1997 lost 60% or more measured in U.S. dollars. That is a real beating and points up the importance of diversification across a number of countries.

Table 6-3

Country Rank
in % Stock Returns
Y/E: 12/31/97

Rank	Country	% Return	Market Size ($ Billions)
1	Turkey	117.1	33.7
2	Hungary	61.8	11.1
3	Mexico	51.6	103.3
4	Portugal	47.8	22.3
5	Switzerland	44.1	465.6
6	Greece	37.7	16.2
7	Italy	35.9	238.9
8	Denmark	34.7	67.7
9	Colombia	34.5	9.1
10	U.S.A.	34.1	6,206.9

Some foreign companies trade on U.S. stock exchanges in U.S. dollars. These are called either **American depositary receipts (ADRs)** or **American depositary shares (ADSs)** and are as easy to purchase as U.S. securities. Also, companies listed as ADRs or ADSs are subject to U.S. accounting standards, which greatly improves the readability of their financial statements for U.S. investors.

When U.S. markets are performing well, some might question the logic of foreign investing. The temptation is great to embrace xenophobia and substitute U.S. companies that have significant foreign sales. Over time, this approach is less likely to improve risk-adjusted returns because you give up the lack of correlation and investing opportunities of foreign stocks. Most U.S. companies are influenced more by the U.S. market in which they are traded than the markets of the foreign countries in which they sell their products or services.

Like their U.S. counterparts, foreign stocks are subject to federal and state income and capital-gains tax. You are credited with any foreign taxes paid if the country of the issuer has a tax treaty with the U.S. The notable exceptions are the Latin American countries, our southern neighbors.

Foreign stocks as an asset class provide you a dramatically expanded set of opportunities for price gains as well as a way to diversify with resultant lower overall risk. Common sense dictates that diversification among countries and regions of the world is very important, particularly in emerging markets.

REAL-ESTATE INVESTMENT TRUSTS

Did you ever walk or drive down a street in the business district of a large city and wonder how anybody scrapes together enough cash to own the great buildings you pass? For many years they typically were owned by either real-estate magnates with deep pockets or institutions like insurance companies and pension funds.

In 1960, a Congressional act created the real-estate investment trust (REIT). A REIT is a tax-exempt corporation that invests in real estate. REITs typically raise equity money in the public capital markets instead of increasing leverage through borrowing. There are three types of REITs. Equity REITs invest in pools of properties that they either own or operate, and they have recently grown dramatically in popularity. Mortgage REITs invest in pools of commercial mortgages; hybrid REITs invest in both. Today, mortgage and hybrid REITs represent a small fraction of all REITs.

Investors own equity REITs for their capital-gain potential as well as current income. Upon sale, REIT shares are subject to federal and state capital-gains tax. Since all REITs are required to distribute 95% of their annual earnings to shareholders, they escape double taxation and have a high yield compared with other equities. This yield is subject to federal and state income tax, but part of it may be tax-deferred. REIT shares offer the small investor access to professionally managed, commercial real-estate investing, which was historically the exclusive turf of large investors and institutions. The values of important commercial properties start well into the millions of dollars, so shares in equity REITs are an effective way to make real estate both affordable and liquid. Equity REITs permit diversification across geographical regions as well as by user classification.

It is easy to imagine that the values of shopping centers, hospitals, industrial warehouses, offices, golf courses and prisons—yes, I said prisons!—might move in patterns that have low cross-correlation. Additionally, REITs have exhibited low to medium correlation to other equities, T-bonds and foreign stocks over longer time horizons.

The main risks with REITs are tenant credit quality, property values and liquidity. Tenant credit quality is very important to review because lease payments provide the bulk of a REIT's cash flow. Property values can rise and fall in response to business conditions, inflation and regional factors. If the properties in a REIT fall sharply in value, its shares will decline and reduce the chance for capital gains. New or smaller REITs are sometimes thinly traded and can be difficult to sell, especially in down markets. All these risks can be reduced to reasonable levels by diversifying the mix of REITs in your portfolio and sticking with proven performers. REITs with a high percentage of founder or management ownership are preferable because in these REITs management's interest is more closely aligned with yours. Investors call this "eating your own cooking." Equity REITs offer an effective way for smaller investors to participate in commercial real estate, an asset class that has low cross-correlation to other asset classes and offers the potential for price gains and high yield.

VARIABLE ANNUITIES

Variable annuities were created by the ever-inventive insurance industry to combine the attraction of investing in equities with the tax-deferral and estate-planning features of insurance. They are a potent response to competition from securities firms and mutual funds for investors' dollars, especially in the retirement and estate-planning arenas. If the insurance products we discussed in the section on debts failed to numb your senses, variable annuities will give you a run for your money. Let's try to get through this without drowning in the details.

Like their fixed-rate cousins, variable annuities are contracts issued by insurance companies to you, the **contract owner**. The contract owner is also normally the investor in a variable annuity. The person whose life measures the length of the contract is called the annuitant. The beneficiary is designated by the owner and receives the proceeds of the entire account upon the death of the **annuitant**, unless the owner has withdrawn it already. Unlike fixed-rate annuities, variable annuities may and do invest in high-octane asset classes like small-cap growth stocks, foreign stocks, REITs, and high-yield corporate bonds. You can tailor the asset-class selections, or **subaccounts**, to match your investment aims and willingness to assume risk. Subaccounts are separate, professionally managed pools of money that focus on a distinct asset class. For example, small-cap stocks, emerging-market stocks, and zero-coupon bonds might be among the choices offered.

You may be inclined to take more investment risk with variable annuities due to a unique feature that they offer. This feature is a guarantee that upon the annuitant's journey to the great beyond, the beneficiary receives the greater of your original investment plus any subsequent contributions or the account value. In effect, the insurance company is saying that no matter what the investment results are in your account, it will pay the beneficiary no less than all the money you invested less any withdrawals. By putting a floor under your investment outcome, you may be less concerned about including higher-volatility asset classes in your subaccounts.

During the annuitant's life, a variable annuity contract provides you with four options:

1. Withdraw all or part of your money
2. Reallocate your money among the issuer's subaccounts
3. Roll over to a new issuer
4. Let it ride until the annuitant expires

Any withdrawal in excess of principal is fully taxable at both the state and federal levels at ordinary rates. Yes, I said ordinary rates! If you withdraw money above a certain percentage of the account balance during the first five to seven years of a contract, you may be subject to a penalty by the issuer. Additionally, if you are under age 59 1/2, the IRS may impose a separate 10% penalty on withdrawals to the extent they are not principal. There are several hardship exceptions to both these possible penalties.

One attractive feature of a variable annuity is the freedom to reallocate your money among subaccounts at no cost. Thus, if your large-cap stocks rise sharply, you can reallocate your gains to other asset classes periodically to restore the percentages that you originally chose. This process is called **rebalancing** and is a good way to buy low and sell high. Don't forget that this is all tax-deferred, so rebalancing does not invite the tax collector to dine at your table until you withdraw gains from your account.

If you become disenchanted with your issuer for any reason, you, the contract owner, may transfer some or all of your account to another qualified issuer. The built-in gain or loss is carried over to the new contract and the new issuer steps into the shoes of the old one. This entire transaction is free from tax under IRS code provision 1035 and is called a **tax-free exchange**. Typical reasons for exercising this choice include poor investment performance, high annual fees, and limited subaccount choices.

If you let the account ride, it compounds tax-deferred during the measuring life of the annuitant. Upon the annuitant's journey to the hereafter, the beneficiary becomes the contract owner and is required to liquidate the account within five years unless he or she is a surviving spouse. A surviving spouse may continue the contract and even rename the beneficiary. This entire process occurs by operation of law and is not subject to probate, the sometimes costly and time-consuming process of validating a will. This spousal exclusion can be a real advantage.

Not surprisingly, all these bells and whistles do not come without a cost. The chief disadvantage of a variable-annuity contract is the tax treatment of withdrawals during liquidation of an account. All withdrawals in excess of principal are fungible from an income-tax perspective. So, if years earlier you made a killing in your stock subaccounts and begin withdrawing from your account on a monthly basis, the gain in excess of principal is fully taxable at your ordinary income-tax rate, not the then-current capital-gains rate. This lack of distinction could cost high-bracket taxpayers up to 19.6% annually (39.6 - 20 = 19.6), the difference between the present federal maximum ordinary rate and long-term capital-gains rate, as well as additional state income tax. Some sellers of variable annuities suggest that your tax bracket probably will decline in your retirement years and render this disadvantage moot. Before purchasing a variable annuity, you should sit down with an independent accountant or adviser and confirm that this rate disadvantage won't come back to bite you in the pocketbook. Another disadvantage of variable annuities is their high fee structure. These include early withdrawal fees, account-maintenance fees and annual fees. Annual fees are in part often sales commissions in disguise under the misnomer **mortality and expense (M&E) risk fee**. Remember, I told you these folks are masterful marketers! It pays to comparison shop features and total fees in investigating variable annuities.

As mentioned before, insurance companies, the issuers of variable annuities, are subject to examination by state regulators and have a nearly spotless track record in honoring payments. This makes them very safe investments. Additionally, they are rated by a number of independent companies, the best known of which is A.M. Best. The Best rating scale of financially secure insurers ranges from a high of A++ to a low of B+. A rating less than B+ is considered financially vulnerable and should be viewed with a jaundiced eye. The issuer's rating should be reviewed periodically, especially prior to purchasing or exchanging a variable annuity.

Variable annuities can be effective investment vehicles if you are prepared to lock away the money for at least 15 to 20 years or until age 59 1/2. By then, the disadvantages will have been offset by the tax-deferred compounding inside the contract. By putting a floor under your investment results, your willingness to assume risk may increase and induce you to select more aggressive subaccounts. Also, if properly used, variable annuities can be retirement and estate-planning tools. I reiterate my exhortation to seek competent, impartial advice before you purchase a contract. Variable-annuity contracts are far from being plain-vanilla and you can receive some nasty surprises if you don't carefully read and fully understand them. Remember this cogent advice: "Everything in the big print will help you; nothing in the fine print will!"

VARIABLE LIFE INSURANCE

As discussed in the section on debts, pure life insurance is really not an investment. It is an income-replacement device that shifts the financial risk of premature death to the insurer. It consists of a contract, or policy, between the insurer and the policyholder that guarantees a stated death benefit will be paid to the beneficiary in exchange for a payment, or premium.

Variable life insurance is permanent, or cash-value. With cash-value insurance you pay a premium that consists of the mortality, or pure life-insurance, portion and an excess that belongs to you, the policyholder. This excess is like a forced savings account that, like variable annuities, can be invested in a selection of subaccounts. The excess compounds tax-deferred, which is another nifty feature that only life insurers can offer, thanks to the great American tradition of lobbying Congress. During the insured's life, the owner may borrow some or all of this excess and its tax-deferred earnings from the policy at a low rate of interest. As long as the policy is in force, these borrowings may be free from tax. While loans are outstanding, canceling the policy can produce a significant taxable event and should be studiously avoided. If the insured relocates to the great beyond while loans are outstanding, the tax-free benefit paid to the beneficiary is reduced by the same amount.

If you genuinely need the income-replacement protection, it can make sense to purchase variable life insurance. It can provide tax-free income from better-performing equity subaccounts. This can be a real advantage over traditional cash-value insurance if you are in a high tax bracket. Be prepared to own the policy for an extended period, so the advantage of tax-deferred compounding within the policy can offset the fees and costs.

As I said before, prior to purchasing any life-insurance product, I urge you to sit down with a competent and impartial adviser and kill yourself on paper. I know this has little appeal, but it is the only way you will stand a ghost of a chance of grasping all the nuances of today's life-insurance products and making an informed comparison. As with annuity contracts, I also urge you to review the rating of the insurer before purchasing variable life insurance. Variable life insurance can have a place in your portfolio if you need the pure income protection, expect to be in a high tax bracket in retirement, and are in it for the long haul. Otherwise, it is unlikely to be a suitable choice for most people.

SUMMARY OF EQUITIES

This completes our discussion of equities. As you can see, the range of choices is broad. As with debts, the key is to match the potential for gain with the risks you are prepared to accept.

7

PEARLS AND PERILS

We have covered most of the good asset classes worthy of our serious consideration as nonprofessional investors. The time now comes to cover the bad and the ugly. We live in a society that relies heavily on the legal concept of *caveat emptor,* or "buyer beware." This concept places the responsibility for making reasonable inquiries about any prospective investment squarely on your shoulders. If you accept verbal, unsubstantiated claims and then sign a written agreement, your legal position is weak unless you can prove that it was more likely than not that you were the victim of fraud.

My pet peeve is receiving phone calls, faxes and **spam** at home from strangers. This is called "dialing for dollars" in the brokerage business, and usually is performed by inexperienced people who are the least capable of providing sound advice. In 30 years of investing, I have never been contacted in any of these ways by a salesperson whose idea was worth hearing. How could he or she possibly know if a product is suitable for a total stranger?

There are a few simple rules that will help you avoid hiring a lawyer to recover your money:

1. Get any investment proposal in writing on the seller's letterhead with a clear explanation of how it works and its risks and rewards.
2. Meet and check out the people involved by calling the state licensing authorities for their line of business or profession.
3. If the investment is unfamiliar and you are still interested, spend a few hundred dollars and hire an impartial professional to walk you through the possible outcomes. This just may be one of the best investments you make.
4. If it still doesn't smell, feel or sound right, walk away.

The following covers investments that I consider poor candidates for your portfolio along with a brief explanation. I realize that some of these might seem like the chance of a lifetime, have enormous appeal to your ego, or feel like the right thing to do, but the fact is they enrich the seller far more often than the buyer.

TANGIBLES

When the inflation rate is rising, clever marketers invariably tout the benefits of **tangible**, or material, assets as a **hedge** against inflation. Tangibles are objects you can touch such as baseball cards, antique furniture, artwork, rare coins, pearls, gemstones and diamonds. Sure, some of this stuff is fun to own, look at and show to your friends, but none of it produces any current income. All of it is sold with a high markup that takes years, if ever, to overcome. Also, the liquidity of these assets is very low if you ever need to raise cash in a hurry. Buy them because you love to own them, not as investments.

THEATER, MUSICALS, AND MOTION PICTURES

A lamb being led to slaughter has a better chance of surviving than you do of making any money in show business. The industry accounting deserves an Oscar for obfuscation, the failure rate is scary, and you stand at the very bottom of the food chain. A former neighbor of mine, who happened to be a very talented surgeon, invested some years ago in a film named *The Giant Spider Invasion* (1975). Needless to say, he probably still suffers from arachnophobia and had yet to show a profit the last time we spoke. If you invest in show business, you will get free tickets, bragging rights and some "A List" invitations to the premiere, but you most likely can say "Good-bye, Mr. Chips" to your hard-earned chips.

PENNY STOCKS AND VENTURE CAPITAL

As their name suggests, penny stocks are dirt cheap. They make you feel like a killing is just around the corner because you can own them for so little. Beware! Penny stocks are not listed on major exchanges and are sold by firms called **market makers** that operate in relative obscurity. They are poorly regulated by the SEC and NASD and given to sales abuses and misrepresentations. The market makers operate on a markup, or **spread**, between the buy and sell price that is usually excessive. When the selling in these stocks takes off, you will find the exit doors either mighty small or closed.

Venture-capital deals typically are based on intellectual property like a patent or scientific research that sounds alluring. There is no track record to examine and the business has usually made little or no sales, so you have no way to judge its prospects or earning power. In venture-capital deals you not only may lose your investment, but also may be called upon to contribute more money to maintain your ownership percentage and keep the business from insolvency. This is called **passing the hat** and can be a nasty surprise.

COMMODITY FUTURES, NAKED OPTIONS, AND SHORT SALES

This group of investments is in a class by itself. All three are the financial equivalent of a minefield at night. If you purchase a debt or stock, you might lose some—or even all—of your initial investment, but never more. With these investments you can lose far more than your investment in a New York minute.

Commodities are animals, plants and minerals that come from, grow on, or feed on the earth. They include cows, pigs, corn, wheat, coffee, gold, platinum and oil. It is hard to imagine buying any of them and taking physical delivery. Your neighbors in downtown Atlanta might object to that herd of Aberdeen Angus grazing in your yard despite their docile and loving nature. Years ago, in response to producers and buyers wishing to lock in the future prices of these commodities, agreements were developed that permit you to contract for future delivery. These are called **futures contracts** and can make good business sense for regular producers and buyers of commodities, but very little sense for you, an investor. Futures contracts belong to a category of financial instruments called **derivatives**. Derivatives derive their value from underlying benchmarks such as foreign-currency rates, interest rates, commodity prices and stock prices.

Through leverage, you can control a large dollar amount of futures contracts with a relatively small investment. That is the good news! The bad news is that you can lose much more than your initial investment if your contract's value drops in response to the underlying commodity price. Your broker will demand you put up additional cash or securities to cover this possibility and will not hesitate to sell them if you receive a notice of deficiency, or **margin call**.

Options are contracts that permit you to control large amounts of stock for a relatively small fee called a **premium**. Like futures contracts, they belong to a category of financial instruments called derivatives. If you believe PachydermWorks' stock price will fall like a stone, you can buy a **put option** that entitles you at a set price to put to the **option writer** 100 or more shares any time during an option period up to a year. If the shares stay at or above the set price, or **strike price**, in value, your contract expires worthless. If the stock price drops below the strike price during the option period, you are in the money and can force the writer to purchase the shares from you at a price above the market. This may result in a profit for you after the cost of the option contract is deducted. Conversely, if you believe PachydermWorks' stock price will rise like a meteor, you can buy a **call option** that entitles you at the strike price to call away from the option writer 100 or more shares any time during an option period up to a year. If the shares stay at or below the strike price in value, your contract expires worthless. If the stock price rises above the strike price during the option period, you are in the money and can force the writer to sell the shares to you at a price below the market. This may result in a profit for you after the cost of the option contract is deducted.

In both these examples, you can never lose more than your initial investment. That is because you were an option buyer, not a writer. If we place the shoe on the other foot and cast you as an option writer, the range of outcomes changes dramatically. If you write options on stock you already own, the risks are limited because your positions are protected by your own stock. These are called **covered options**. If you write options on stock you do not already own, the risks are theoretically unlimited. These are called **naked options**.

Let's say you are convinced PachydermWorks' stock price is overvalued at $70 and you write a naked call option on 1,000 shares for three months at a strike price of $75. The premium you collect is, say, $2 a share, or $2,000 (1,000 x 2 = 2,000). Four weeks later, PachydermWorks announces it has developed a new technology that can identify spousal prevarication in males with a hand-held voice analyzer. At the same time, the company announces it has inked an agreement to sell these units on the *Dr. Laura Show* and projects sales in the millions of units. The stock takes off and trades up to $115 within a month. Although you have disconnected your phone and left no forwarding address, a registered letter finds its way to your remote cabin on the scenic coast of Greenland. It contains a margin call and informs you that your loss stands at $40,000. This is arrived at by taking the 1,000 shares times the $40 (115 - 75 = 40) loss per share (1,000 x 40 = 40,000). As you can see, your best-case profit in this naked call is the entire premium of $2,000. You have managed to lose $38,000 (40,000 - 2,000 = 38,000), or 19 times, more than you could ever make. Therein lies the peril of writing naked options.

If you are convinced a stock is overvalued and will fall, you can sell it. Believe it or not, you can even sell it if you don't own it by temporarily borrowing it from an owner who is prepared to lend it to you. This is called a **short sale** and can produce really large, but finite, gains. The best outcome you can hope for is that the stock goes south to zero. You will, however, need to open a **margin account** in which you place cash or securities in the event your shorted stock heads north. If your shorted stock heads north, you will pay daily interest and be exposed to margin calls as your account equity is systematically wiped out. You can always say "uncle," buy the shorted stock at the market price, and return it to the lender. This is called **covering** your position. Alternatively, you can stubbornly maintain your short position and keep adding equity to your margin account. Theoretically, your loss potential is infinite because the shorted stock can rise without limit.

Wait! Listen! It gets even uglier because when you finally give up and bid for the shorted stock to return it to the lender, you increase demand, which drives up the price even further. This is called a **short squeeze** and gives you one final chance to shoot yourself in the foot before you unwind the short sale. If that isn't scary, I don't know what is! I think you can see by now why these investments are in a class by themselves.

LIMITED PARTNERSHIPS

Limited partnerships (LPs) typically are formed by investment houses or **syndicators** as investment vehicles that offer you access to businesses and tax benefits not otherwise available to small investors. For example, LPs often are formed to own and operate properties in oil and gas, cable television, equipment leasing, and commercial real estate. These businesses can depreciate their qualifying long-term assets, which reduces taxable income in your hands. These businesses require industry-specific expertise, which is furnished by the general partners, who are legally liable for the acts of the LP. You, the investor, are called a limited partner because your legal liability is limited to your investment. You also may be asked to sign notes that you could be called upon to honor personally in the future. These would add to your investment and are called **recourse notes**.

In some cases, LPs perform just fine and you receive your projected return and tax benefits. In the majority of cases, LPs fall far short of delivering the projected results. The main disadvantages and risks of LPs are listed below:

1. High up-front fees and sales commissions
2. Lack of limited partners' say in LP governance
3. Lack of liquidity except in very few cases
4. Long time horizon of investment, which locks you in
5. Additional financial risk through recourse notes
6. Federal tax reform that guts the tax benefits

I don't know how you feel, but when I see a list of negatives this long, no further study is required. I suggest that if you are powerfully attracted to an industry, you do some homework and identify public companies in that or a related field. Substituting common stock in the same industry for an LP investment can be a very wise move. You might miss out on some of the tax and other promised benefits, but your list of negatives will be far shorter than the one above.

VIATICAL SETTLEMENTS

Viatical is derived from the Latin word *viaticum*, which means a provision for a journey such as money, clothing or food. In Roman Catholicism, *Viaticum* also means Holy Communion for those *in extremis*. Viatical settlements are legal agreements in which a terminally ill insured assigns to a viatical company the right to collect his or her life-insurance death benefit in exchange for a discounted amount of immediate cash. The viatical company then sells at a profit the policy—or packages of several policies—to an investor. The insured, or **viator**, benefits because he or she is able to use the immediate cash during life. The investor benefits because the insurance proceeds, when paid, may yield an attractive fixed annual return that is predicated on the insured's life expectancy.

Viatical settlements have become increasingly prevalent in the last decade as people afflicted with AIDS and cancer have discovered that assigning their death benefits can provide them with much-needed cash for their final months. There is no doubt that such arrangements allow the terminally ill to monetize life-insurance benefits at a time of great need, which may have great appeal to investors who are sensitive to humanitarian needs. However, for the investor there are a number of significant risks:

1. The actual yield may be less than projected if the viator outlives the life expectancy that was projected.
2. New therapies and/or drugs may increase dramatically the viator's life expectancy.
3. The investor may become responsible for the insurance premiums, if the viator is unable to pay them.
4. The two-year **contestability period** of the viator's policy may not have expired, in which case the insurer may not pay a death benefit if fraudulent or misleading statements were made on the policy application.
5. According to a 1996 federal appeals court decision, viatical settlements are not securities. Hence, the viatical industry flies under the radar of federal licensing and regulatory bodies. Additionally, few states regulate the industry.
6. Viatical settlements are illiquid due to the lack of an active secondary market.
7. An investor could lose his or her entire investment if the settlement company goes out of business.

In theory, investing in viatical settlements is a win-win situation and serves an important social need, but the industry is highly fragmented and largely unregulated. Until viatical settlements become mainstream investment vehicles, I recommend that you avoid them and substitute high-yield bonds in your portfolio.

SUMMARY OF PEARLS AND PERILS

If you found this chapter decidedly negative, you understood it correctly. There are plenty of opportunities for investing success in the good asset classes; you don't need to venture into the bad and the ugly. If you choose to ignore this admonition, *caveat emptor*!

8

MUTUAL FUNDS

If you think the financial-product designers at insurance companies are smart, wait until you learn how a few visionaries like John Bogle, Ned Johnson and Sir John Templeton reinvented investing. They saw the American public's appetite for investing, the lack of access to professional advisers, and the high capital requirement of sound diversification as unmet needs. Their response was to form investment companies that, for a fee, pooled client assets, diversified, and invested with a purpose. This seemingly simple idea's time had come and they capitalized on it brilliantly and lucratively. The rest is history! In the last 25 years, the U.S. mutual-fund industry has grown from a relatively obscure area of investing to a financial juggernaut with **assets under management (AUM)** over $5 trillion in some 11,000 funds. As the baby boomers save for retirement and businesses all across the country eschew traditional pension plans, mutual funds have become the investing vehicle of choice for millions of Americans. At the end of 1997, AUM of all U.S. mutual funds rapidly was approaching the total dollars in the U.S. banking system. That is stunning!

Successful mutual-fund companies with increasing AUMs can be very profitable businesses due to **economies of scale** and fee growth. Take a look at the performance of Franklin Resources, the acquiror of the Templeton Funds Group. Its **ticker symbol** is BEN and it has returned over 34% compounded annually for the five years ended March 31, 1998. Using the rule of 72, you can see that this stock almost has doubled every two years (72/34 = 2.12) since March 1993. It doesn't get much better than that!

Strictly speaking, mutual funds are investment companies, which are regulated by the Investment Company Act of 1940. They come in two basic forms. The first is **open-end**, or mutual, which sells shares at **net asset value (NAV)** to as many investors as the fund management chooses. NAV per share is calculated daily by dividing the net assets of the fund by the number of shares. Some open-end funds elect to close to new investors after reaching a certain size; others do not and keep growing. The second basic form of investment company is **closed-end**, which acts much like a corporation. Closed-end funds issue a limited number of shares that are traded like a stock in the secondary market. The assets under management of a closed-end fund are fixed and the fund does not accept additional contributions from investors after its initial offering. The share price is not based strictly on NAV, but rather on how the market feels about the management and the portfolio. Closed-end funds can trade at a premium or a discount to NAV at any given time. Additionally, closed-end funds typically have more liberal investment rules and frequently are permitted to use leverage. The use of leverage can enhance returns, but also can increase risk.

In recent years, another type of pooled-investment vehicle that resembles a closed-end fund has been sponsored increasingly by large brokerage firms. It is called a unit investment trust (UIT). UITs invest with a limited life span in an unmanaged, fixed portfolio of securities such as bonds, stocks or REITs. Most UITs are thematic and target a specific area or theory such as the "Dow Dogs," which is based on the notion that investors will be rewarded for owning the ten highest-yielding stocks in the **Dow Jones industrial average (DJIA)**. The UIT sponsor sells units in the trust, which you either can redeem with the sponsor for close to NAV or hold to maturity. During the UIT's life, you receive any investment income it produces. At maturity, the UIT is dissolved, and you receive your share of the trust in cash. A disadvantage with UITs is their high sales fees, which are recurring because they must be replaced periodically due to their short lives.

The debts and equities we discussed in the previous chapters represent all the available asset classes and the individual securities that each asset class contains. There are no others. Collectively, these are called the global investing **universe**. Mutual-fund companies select their securities from the very same universe you and I do. What makes them unique are the following features:

1. Professional management
2. Specific investment focus, or style
3. Diversification
4. Low minimum investment requirement
5. Liquidity
6. Reasonable fees, in most cases
7. Customer service

These are powerful features that make it possible for you to build a diversified portfolio with a relatively small amount of capital. Let's take a closer look at these aspects of mutual funds. Professional management is the major advantage of owning mutual funds. The mutual-fund companies identify, recruit and develop very talented people to act as fund managers. Successful managers like Peter Lynch, Michael Price and George Soros have achieved celebrity status in the investment community. Their opinions are highly sought and when they speak, most everyone listens! Fund managers are among the highest-paid folks in the business, but the pressure to produce persistent, superior results is tremendous. If they do not, they may find themselves occupants of an organizational dark star in a big hurry. Therefore, the tenure and success of the fund manager is a critical consideration in selecting a mutual fund.

Every mutual fund has a focus, or style, that is the central theme of its investing strategy. This style is described in the fund's prospectus and is important for you to read and understand. If the fund's security holdings, which typically are revealed only twice a year in the semiannual and annual reports, do not square with the stated style, the fund may be experiencing **style drift**. Style drift can be a warning to you that the manager has lost his or her conviction and bears further investigation. By the way, relying on the fund's name to identify its style is hazardous. Fidelity Magellan, the largest U.S.-equity mutual fund with nearly $70 billion under management on April 1, 1998, is not even remotely international despite the Portuguese origin and circumnavigatory prowess of its namesake Ferdinand Magellan.

Mutual-fund styles represent a triumph of the human imagination! With over 10,000 funds in the U.S alone, you would think that the industry would be fresh out of new ideas. Think again! Apart from the traditional asset classes, you can invest in **training-wheel funds** for novice investors, **socially responsible funds** for conscientious investors, **market-neutral funds** for ambivalent investors, and **funds-of-funds** for imperial investors, to name a few. The main fund styles are defined and classified by statistical service firms like Lipper, Inc. and Morningstar, Inc. These firms slice and dice debt, equity and all other mutual funds into categories, or **peer groups**. For instance, Lipper, Inc. divides debt and equity mutual funds into 55 and 34 peer groups, respectively. Both Lipper and Morningstar rank funds within and among the peer groups by AUM, return, risk and expense ratio over various time frames. This information can be very helpful in selecting individual funds to buy or sell in your portfolio based on your expectations about return and your willingness to assume risk. It is available on the Internet, in financial publications and from your fund distributor, broker or adviser.

Diversification is another compelling feature of mutual funds. Modern portfolio theory holds that about a third of the risk of owning an individual security is related to the market in general. This is called **systematic risk**. The balance of the risk is specific to that individual security. This is called **unsystematic risk**. By investing in a mutual fund that owns 30 or more securities, you can virtually eliminate unsystematic risk. This means that for as little as $500 you can expect the same relative risk and return as an investor who commits to owning 30 or more securities. Now, that's powerful! Many mutual funds have a minimum investment requirement of as little as $500; others start at $2,500 and up. As we just discovered, this is a very small amount compared to the capital needed to own an equally diversified portfolio of individual securities. Owning 100 shares of 30 different stocks with an average price per share of $35 would easily cost over $100,000 (100 x 30 x 35 = 105,000). Mutual funds permit you to invest like a professional on a budget.

All open-end and most closed-end mutual-fund shares are highly liquid. From time to time, closed-end shares trading at a premium can be hard to sell and, therefore, less liquid. This is because little demand may exist for closed-end shares priced well above their underlying NAV.

Mutual-fund fees fall into two basic categories. The first, which is charged by all funds, relates to the ongoing costs and expenses of paying the managers, buying and selling securities, customer service, audit fees, and the like. These operating expenses are deducted from fund assets and directly reduce NAV. Generally, debt funds have lower management fees than equity funds because security selection is less costly to execute. The second basic category is sales expense, which is paid to compensate the advisers, brokers and agents who sell you the fund. Sales expense can be deducted from your contribution before it is invested in the fund or upon early withdrawal; alternatively, it can be deducted from NAV on an ongoing basis. This latter type is called a rule 12b-1 fee after an arcane SEC regulation. Additionally, some funds may charge **redemption fees**, **reinvestment fees** and **exchange fees** as set forth in the prospectus.

Funds that only charge operating expenses are called **no-load funds**. No-load funds are sold directly to you by the fund company. The cost of no-load funds is usually significantly cheaper because there is no sales commission, but you must be willing to research them by yourself or hire an investment adviser to assist you. Funds that charge both operating and sales expenses are called **load funds**. Load funds are sold by a variety of advisers, brokers and agents who earn fees or commissions for their services. Load-fund shares often are divided further into classes based on their fee structure. Class A shares are generally front-end load with sales commissions taken out of your contributions. Class B shares are generally back-end load with early surrender fees taken out of your sales proceeds if you exit the fund within five years. These surrender fees decline over time to zero. Class C shares are generally free of sales load and are used in adviser relationships called **wrap programs**, in which you pay an annual fee to a professional financial adviser. Class B and C shares usually charge higher ongoing fees to compensate for the loss of the front-end load.

This is the single area of mutual funds that leads me to wonder if they hired the inventive folks who thought up variable annuities. The fee structures for load funds have gone from utter simplicity to a Byzantine morass of complex choices. It really pays to mind the fees and walk through the share classes to see which fund and class works best in your situation. Generally speaking, class A shares are most effective for very long investment horizons because the ongoing fees are lower. Conversely, class B shares are more effective for short and medium investment horizons since you defer paying the piper until you exit the fund.

Customer service is also an attractive feature of mutual funds. Most funds have Web sites and 800 numbers that connect you to customer-service representatives. Additionally, fund companies provide audited financial statements, supply tax information, and collect and disburse or reinvest your investment income. Open-end companies with multiple funds also may provide exchange privileges among their family of funds at low or no cost. This privilege allows you to call the company and move money from one fund to another to reposition your portfolio. Bear in mind that an exchange within a fund family is treated as a taxable event by the IRS unless the exchange occurs in a tax-deferred account.

The disadvantages of mutual funds are only two. The first is the complete delegation of the investment process to a stranger, the fund manager. Talking directly to fund managers is limited to very large investors and their advisers. You probably will never see or speak to one in person. If the manager underperforms, you are stuck with those results. All you can do is fire the manager by selling your shares and pick a new fund. I cannot overemphasize the importance of investigating the tenure and track record of a fund's manager before you send in your hard-earned money. The fund's prospectus, customer-service department and Web site are good places to start. The second disadvantage is the loss of control you exercise over income taxes compared to individual securities, which you can hold or sell as your tax situation dictates. Fund managers are measured and compensated on their investment performance before taxes. This can motivate them to seek the highest quarterly and annual returns possible regardless of trading activity, or turnover. If your shares are held in a fully taxable account, you may pay more taxes sooner by owning shares in a high-turnover fund. This is especially true today with the maximum long-term capital-gains rate at 20%. When considering a fund for a fully taxable account, the turnover and percentage of capital gains held 12 months or longer can provide valuable insights into the fund's tax-efficiency.

Mutual funds are required to distribute annually substantially all of their income and **realized gains**. This typically occurs in the fourth quarter. It is almost never wise to purchase shares just prior to a distribution if your account is subject to tax. You will receive almost immediately a partial return of your investment on which you will owe tax. Nice shot to the foot, partner!

There is a movement afoot to pressure mutual-fund companies to adopt **highest-in, first-out (HIFO)** accounting. Remember our discussion on cost-flow assumptions in the section on accounting? This is another example of electing a cost-flow assumption that impacts income determination.

There are two remaining questions for you to consider as you evaluate mutual funds. The first is whether you would be served better by owning individual securities, mutual funds or a combination of both. Investing in individual securities takes a great deal more effort on your or your adviser's part in performing research and monitoring company performance. You are, in effect, the fund manager and must perform on a small scale the very same set of tasks a mutual-fund manager performs. If you have the time, interest and ability, investing partly or completely in individual securities can be an engrossing and rewarding activity. It also can be more tax-efficient since you are free to consider only your own tax position. The second question is whether to invest in actively managed or "eyes-closed" mutual funds. Actively managed funds employ a manager who seeks to beat the market index over time through security selection and timing. "Eyes-closed," or index, funds buy all the securities in an index, say, the S&P 500, and mimic its return. The actively managed funds that periodically outperform the market index tout their investing skills and often charge higher fees for the promise of an encore performance. The index funds claim that they consistently outperform 80% of all similarly tilted funds, so why bother with active management and its higher fees? Additionally, the indexers point to far lower turnover and resultant deferral of taxes since they only infrequently replace holdings in response to changes in the index composition.

There are no cut-and-dried answers to these questions. It is up to you to decide if active management is worth the additional cost in fees and taxes. Mutual funds that consistently outperform their index are few and far between, but they do exist. Many academicians would argue that seeking them is a **Sisyphean** undertaking. To paraphrase Joseph Schumpeter, the brilliant economist, the hotel rooms of outperformance are always full, but they're full with different people.

Mutual funds are an ingenious and effective way to reach a variety of asset classes with professional management, elimination of unsystematic risk, and small amounts of capital. When evaluating a mutual fund, the absolute and risk-adjusted performance record of the manager, its tax-efficiency, and the expenses and sales load of the fund are important considerations.

9

THE PLAYERS

The investment arena never has had a more confusing cast of characters than is present today. The legal walls, which were erected during the **Great Depression** of the 1930s between securities firms, banks and insurance companies, are crumbling. What's more, everybody and his or her brother and sister seems to be hawking securities, mutual funds and insurance products while posing as accountants, advisers, bankers, consultants, money managers, planners and trust officers. At times, you may feel like Diogenes of Sinope, the philosopher, whose diurnal wanderings with a lantern about ancient Athens seeking an honest person made him a poster boy for cynicism. Let's try to restore some order to this proliferating morass.

The investment business can be divided broadly into the buy side and the sell side. The buy side includes all the individuals, firms, companies and institutions that purchase securities for their own or client accounts. They are all investors and are enriched only if their portfolios increase in value or they collect management fees.

Everyone else belongs to the sell side. They do not own securities except as inventory held for resale and are enriched by sales commissions or advisory fees. Regardless of what they call themselves, these are the folks whose job it is to sell you financial products. In many cases, these are also the indefatigable folks who could find your phone number even if you were in the Federal Witness Protection Program in Caledonia, Illinois. Believe me, some are that persistent, and that good! The main players in today's investment arena and their distinguishing features are discussed below.

STOCKBROKERS

Stockbrokers, or brokers, are the registered representatives of firms that sell securities to individuals like you and me. We are considered retail clients in contrast to large, institutional clients. Brokers must satisfy national and state licensing requirements before they are permitted to engage in the business. For many years, all brokerage firms were full-service and had fixed commission schedules. Broker selection was based primarily on personal preference and the financial strength and reputation of the firm. Brokers are usually compensated by splitting sales commissions on all security trades with their firm. The broker typically receives about 40% of the total commission. More recently, some brokers have offered annual contracts called wrap programs under which they collect a fee based on a percentage of your AUM. In recent years, deregulation of commissions has spawned a whole new set of choices including low-service and Internet brokerage firms. They are called **discount brokers** and often have very low commission schedules, as their name suggests. At the same time, they have lower service levels, so you must make the trade-off between cost and service based on your needs.

The NASD maintains a Central Registration Depository (CRD) that contains disciplinary data about all registered representatives. Unfortunately, the CRD does not reveal pending complaints, complaints settled in arbitration, or convictions on appeal. Your best bet in checking out a broker is to contact the securities regulator of the state in which the broker is licensed.

INSURANCE AGENTS

Insurance agents are the retail sales force of insurance companies. They must be licensed in the state in which they do business. As we saw in the sections on fixed and variable annuities, insurance products are highly complex and require patience and knowledge to sell. Many agents possess these skills and do a fine job. However, the industry has a history of convincing clients to switch from an existing product to a newer one with different and better features. This can be costly to you in fees and commissions, so obtain an impartial opinion from a professional before you make a switch. Insurance companies are rated by independent services like A.M. Best. These ratings are important to consider when selecting an insurance product since your contract is with the company not the agent.

You can check out an agent's license and disciplinary history by contacting your state insurance commissioner. Bear in mind that many agents represent a single insurer, so their objectivity may be suspect. Insurance is an area in which comparison shopping is very important.

FINANCIAL PLANNERS

The ranks of financial planners have grown steadily in the last ten years. Planners hold themselves out as able to handle your financial needs from womb to tomb. They come in two basic varieties. The first is commissioned; the second is fee-only. Commissioned planners usually sell specific products such as open-end mutual funds or annuities. They have relationships with distributors and issuers who pay them sales commissions and are often loath to offer other, competing products. Some investors worry that their advice is potentially biased because of that limitation. Fee-only planners usually develop an investment plan and let the client purchase the investments through a stockbroker, insurance agent or no-load mutual-fund company. They are compensated by fees based on either hours spent or AUM. Some investors feel that their advice is impartial because they are paid by the client. The three main designations for professionally accredited planners are:

1. Certified Financial Planner (CFP)
2. Chartered Financial Consultant (ChFC)
3. Personal Financial Specialist (PFS)

CERTIFIED PUBLIC ACCOUNTANTS

Certified Public Accountants (CPAs) are required to meet state licensing requirements and pass a rigorous national examination. Traditionally, CPAs specialized in auditing and tax services for both individuals and businesses. More recently, they have expanded their practices to include management-information services and personal-financial planning. Although their basic training is not focused heavily on investing, many CPAs have taken additional courses in investing and related subjects. CPAs usually are compensated by hourly fees and, in a steadily declining number of states, are prohibited from receiving commissions. As these barriers fall, mutual-fund companies seeking additional distribution channels increasingly woo CPAs to promote and sell their products.

CPAs often have access to the intimate details of your finances, so they are in a good position to provide personalized investment advice. They are also good candidates for crunching the numbers and rendering impartial advice on complex investments like life insurance, annuities and tax-deferred retirement vehicles.

TRUST OFFICERS

Trust officers are the professional employees of trust companies, which are regulated by the U.S. Comptroller of the Currency. Trust companies are the platform that many banks use to participate in fee-based estate and trust administration and money management for clients. They also act as safekeepers, or **custodians**, of client assets managed by others and as gatekeepers for other services such as estate planning, tax preparation and brokerage. Trust companies manage both individual portfolios and common trust funds for clients. Despite a historical reputation for archconservatism in investing, studies indicate that in recent years, bank-managed portfolios of both debts and equities have performed as well as similarly tilted portfolios of mutual-fund companies and investment-advisory firms. Incidentally, bank-managed portfolios carry the same market risks as nonbank portfolios and are not guaranteed against loss of principal. Since trust companies act as **fiduciaries**, their employees are held to the highest standard of conduct under the law. Additionally, most carry a large amount of **errors and omissions (E&O) insurance**, which provides clients an added measure of security.

MONEY MANAGERS

Money managers frequently are called investment advisers or investment counselors. They are the folks whom institutions and high-net-worth individuals hire to supervise separately managed accounts. They operate at the top of the financial food chain and typically have minima in the range of $250 thousand and up per account. In most cases, they earn a fee based solely on AUM. Some of the more exotic money managers like **hedge-fund** specialists also may earn performance fees after a certain threshold, or **high-water mark**, has been exceeded. The business is focused heavily on institutional investors like pension funds, insurance companies, charitable foundations and endowment funds. Some money managers also provide advisory services under contract to mutual funds. If you have sufficient capital to meet their minima, money managers can tailor portfolios to your specifications. Most have a single investment style, or expertise, for which they are best known. Hence, a diversified investment program typically includes several or more money managers to cover all the asset classes.

CONSULTANTS

Consultants are hired often by institutions and other large investors to select and ride herd over their money managers. Consultants are investing strategists and do not participate in the tactical investment process. They assist clients in developing written investment objectives and policy, performing asset-allocation studies, conducting manager searches and measuring portfolio risk and performance. Some consultants have developed computer software that audits client portfolios to ensure that securities are properly priced and that all purchases, sales and income are properly and timely posted. This can add reliability to reporting, especially in large or complex portfolios where the cost of error is high. Consultants typically charge an annual fee for their services and historically have limited their activities to pure consulting to avoid conflicts of interest. Competent, impartial consultants can add considerable value to a client's investment program.

CHARTERED FINANCIAL ANALYSTS

Chartered Financial Analysts (CFAs) are among the academic heavyweights in the investing arena. The CFA designation is granted by the Association of Investment Management and Research (AIMR) after candidates complete a very rigorous educational program. The CFA designation carries great weight in the investment community. Their ranks are a who's who of important money managers and investment professionals. AIMR also develops and promulgates the performance-reporting standards that money managers and consultants should follow. New AIMR standards took effect in 1993 and represent the state of the art in investment-performance reporting on a uniform and meaningful basis.

REGISTERED INVESTMENT ADVISERS

Anyone not otherwise licensed who professionally dispenses investment advice, including financial planners, CPAs, money managers, consultants and CFAs, is required to register with either the SEC or the state in which he or she practices as a Registered Investment Adviser (RIA). RIAs must complete annually a **Form ADV** parts I and II, which discloses their disciplinary record, business practices and fee structure. RIAs are subject to SEC regulatory scrutiny and audit if their AUMs exceed $25 million. Except in Ohio and Wyoming, which are still regulated by the SEC, all smaller RIAs are subject to regulatory scrutiny at the state level. I urge you to request and review Form ADV because it contains a wealth of useful information. RIAs are regulated very loosely due to their sheer numbers. For example, the SEC only has some 50 regulators to monitor the approximately 7,000 RIAs whose AUMs exceed the $25 million threshold. Additionally, there is currently no competency test that RIAs must pass in order to open up shop. In some states it requires a greater demonstration of competence to become a barber than a money manager. Now, that's a hair-raising state of affairs!

SUMMARY OF THE PLAYERS

All of the above categories include people who range from freshly minted rookies with good intentions to real pros with considerable investing savvy. Like any other area of commerce, there are also a few bad apples in the barrel. In selecting investment professionals, it is just as important to ask for their experience and performance record as their academic and professional credentials. If advanced degrees alone determined investing success, the savants would have all the money already.

Investment professionals have a variety of compensation schemes, so it is helpful to relate your total annual expenses to some base. I prefer to use AUM as a base because it is easy to understand and provides an incentive for the adviser to increase the client's wealth. Keep in mind that management fees for debts are typically lower than similar fees for equities. In larger, diversified portfolios, expenses should run about 150 basis points (1.5%). Total annual expenses in smaller portfolios, say, under $250,000, may run as high as 250 basis points, or 2.5%. Total expenses are particularly important if your portfolio contains a high debt allocation since they can really burn down your effective yield. For instance, if annual expenses run 100 basis points, or 1%, and your portfolio yields 6.5% annually, your effective yield before taxes is reduced by 15% (1/6.5 = .15). Equity investors are usually less sensitive to expenses because they represent a smaller piece of the return. However, in down markets, annual expenses stand out like a sore thumb. Nobody enjoys paying for the privilege of making losses.

Nothing speaks more loudly about a professional's skill than positive recommendations from other clients with similar investment objectives. I urge you to ask any professional you are considering to provide you with relevant references. It also pays to check out any professional with the federal or state licensing or regulating authority to which he or she is subject. It is also useful to interview several professionals within the same area of expertise before making a final decision. After all, you are entrusting him or her with your financial future. During the interview process, be sure to develop a feel for your level of comfort with each candidate. His or her sincerity and ability to listen are important attributes in an advisory relationship. At the end of the day, you are right back to *caveat emptor*, so do your homework diligently and pick the members of your investment team with great care.

10

Economic and Market Statistics

READING

With the possible exception of professional athletics, there probably is no single activity about which more statistics are produced than the economy and the financial markets. They are cranked out daily by the boatload in both the public and private sectors and recycled *ad nauseam* in the printed and electronic media. Most investors regard this deluge of information as a distraction from the pursuit of successful, long-term investing. The acid test for the value of information is whether learning it would change your course of action. Most information you read and hear abysmally fails this test. Pareto's Law suggests that you should be selective, focusing on that 20% or less of information that is useful to your decision making. I have found that only 20 minutes a day of speed-reading a small number of publications can be perfectly adequate to remain informed. If an article or piece captures your attention, circle or highlight it and read it more carefully as time permits. You may have a favorite spot to read in serene, undisturbed surroundings. I do, but I'm not telling where. In many cases, a visit to an

Internet Web site on business can replace daily publications provided that you are not afflicted with **logizomechanophobia**. My suggestions for your minimum daily reading follow.

LOCAL NEWSPAPER

The front page and business section of your local newspaper can keep you up to speed on matters of local economic importance. If you simply must look up your investment holdings in the debt and stock tables, go ahead, but don't count it as productive time. The same goes for Little League scores and *Dilbert*.

NATIONAL OR INTERNATIONAL NEWSPAPER

You should subscribe to one world-class newspaper. The *Wall Street Journal*, the *New York Times*, the *Herald Tribune* or the *Financial Times*, among others, will do just fine. Armed with the knowledge contained in this book, these papers are very readable and give you an international perspective. Remember, well over half of all investment opportunities reside in other countries.

PERIODICALS

There are more magazines, journals, newsletters and instructional videos floating around than ever before. The fine folks who publish them earn their livelihood solely from subscription and advertising revenues. Stop and think about it for a minute! If they really had information guaranteed to make a killing in the market, would they suffer a crisis of conscience and share it with you in Alpharetta, Georgia? Of course not! They would guard it with their lives and become richer than **Croesus**.

Consider confining your periodical reading to publications that increase your investment knowledge and avoid perishable news that has little lasting value. I am very impressed by the American Association of Individual Investors (AAII) in Chicago, Illinois (Web site: www.aaii.com). The *AAII Journal* is manageable reading and focuses heavily on investor education. The AAII also offers other valuable services and the price is right.

The financial reports and comments issued by the securities and mutual funds that you either own or are considering for purchase are mandatory reading. Even if you scan them, the contents provide insight into the ongoing ability of the investment to deserve a place in your portfolio. Incidentally, you may have to notify the custodian or broker who safekeeps your debt and stock certificates to forward the issuer communications if they are registered in the custodian's name. If time is limited, place them in a pile and read them on the weekend or during a business trip. The information has a useful life of several weeks or more, so periodic reading is just fine.

Well, that's it! You don't have to be a voracious reader or listener to keep current. Just be selective and stick with what works for you.

INDICATORS

Economic and financial-market statistics, or data, can be divided into two categories. Macroeconomic data describe the broad picture of the national economy and the interrelationships among its sectors. Microeconomic data describe the far narrower picture of the forces that affect a single business or industry. Sell-side Wall Street firms employ highly trained economists who use economic data to build sophisticated, computerized forecasting models. When reading their forecasts, bear in mind this simple rule: If all the economists in the world were placed end to end, they would not reach agreement. The main flaw in forecasting lies in recognizing significant departures from historical patterns. America's economic rejuvenation as the leading global supplier of information technology was grossly underestimated. Similarly, the confluence of low inflation, baby boomers' investment-accumulation habits, and a balanced federal budget, which has propelled the U.S. equity markets to nosebleed territory, was not foreseen. Precious few prognosticators bat much over .500. Even the Psychic Network, that late-night television tribute to viewer gullibility, failed to foresee its own demise as it recently filed for bankruptcy.

I try to keep an eye on the following generally available macroeconomic data about the U.S. and any other developed country in which I own individual securities.

INFLATION

Inflation rates are measured in several ways. The CPI measures inflation's impact on consumers like you and me. The producer price index (PPI) measures inflation's impact on producers who purchase materials, services and labor and usually leads the CPI. Inflation is meaningful to investors in calculating real returns.

GROSS DOMESTIC PRODUCT

This measures the sum total of all goods and services produced by a nation. It is a way of ranking countries by the size of their economies and discerning growth trends.

UNEMPLOYMENT

This measure is self-explanatory and measures the percentage of able-bodied people actively seeking work. Low unemployment can fuel wage inflation. High unemployment can indicate a slowing of economic activity, mortgage and consumer-loan defaults, and increased demand for government safety-net services. The unemployment rate is sometimes added to the inflation rate to produce the so-called misery index, a decidedly negative measure.

FEDERAL BUDGET DEFICIT

Unlike you and me, federal governments can spend themselves into oblivion and issue debt to cover the shortfalls. The federal budget deficit or surplus can be a good indicator of national fiscal policy and management. Most stable, national economies have their budgets under tight control. The recently projected U.S. federal budget surplus is good news, especially for the Social Security System, which so many Americans depend on during retirement.

EXCHANGE RATES

Exchange rates can be important determinants of a nation's supply and demand patterns. If the U.S. dollar is strong, we Americans scurry to import foreign goods because they look cheap to us. Meanwhile, American exporters suffer. Conversely, if the U.S. dollar is weak, foreign nations scurry to import our American goods because they look cheap to them. Meanwhile, American importers suffer. One venerable periodical, the *Economist,* has even devised a lighthearted foreign-currency valuation model based on the theory of purchasing-power parity (PPP) among countries. PPP holds that an identical basket of goods and services should cost the same in all countries. The valuation model compares the cost of a Big Mac sandwich in the PPP-adjusted local currency of various countries and draws conclusions about the correctness of their valuation levels relative to the U.S. dollar. It is called the Big Mac index. I suspect its faithful followers are few. Exchange rates are also indicators of international confidence in a country, its prospects and stability.

INTEREST RATES

There are all sorts of different interest rates. The interest rates most relevant to investors are found in the sovereign, or treasury, yield curve. It shows the risk-free rates across all maturities and serves as a guide, or benchmark, for debt owners. These rates are driven in large part by central bankers who fine-tune their national economies through monetary policy. Interest rates also impact capital flows among nations as fixed-income investors pursue yield on a global basis.

The Federal Reserve Bank is our central banking mechanism. Its policy committee, the present chairman of which is Alan Greenspan, has been an important stabilizing influence on U.S. capital markets for several decades. William McChesney Martin, the longest-serving chairman of the policy committee in history, once said the role of the central bank was to "take away the punch bowl just when the party gets going." Monetary policy really can exert that degree of influence on capital markets.

STOCK-MARKET INDEX

Every developed stock market has a published index that tracks its general price level. For example, U.S. investors look to the S&P 500 or the DJIA, British investors look to the Financial Times 100 and Japanese investors look to the Nikkei index. Glancing at these from time to time can keep you abreast of general market conditions and trends.

STOCK-MARKET-INDEX **P/E**

The P/E of any stock market's index is an important valuation indicator. It shows the level at which the market as a whole is priced. The present S&P 500 P/E is above 26 times 1997 operating earnings, which is record territory. Prospectively, the current S&P 500 P/E is above 20 times forecast 1998 operating earnings, but that is only a forecast and can vary widely from actual results. Tracking their index P/Es can give you a feel for how dearly or cheaply different markets are priced.

STOCK-MARKET-INDEX EARNINGS YIELD

The earnings yield of any stock market's index is the inverse of the P/E. It often is compared to the yield of the 30-year sovereign or T-bond as an indicator of relative valuation. Stocks are riskier than government bonds, so you might expect the index earnings yield to be higher than the long T-bond yield. If it is not, some investors feel that a correction in stock prices is imminent. On the other hand, more optimistic investors feel that high corporate-earnings growth rates can justify this apparent imbalance. The present S&P 500-index earnings yield is under 4% based on 1997 earnings while the long T-bond yields nearly 6%.

STOCK-MARKET-INDEX DIVIDEND YIELD

The dividend yield of any stock market's index shows the relationship between annual dividends and the market price per share. If share prices rise faster than the dividend, the yield drops. Presently, the S&P 500 dividend yield is at a historical low of 1.4%. As recently as 1992, the yield was nearly 3%. Value investors like dividend yield and feel it cushions stock prices in declining markets. Growth investors are indifferent to dividend yield and feel companies can find better uses for cash such as acquisitions and repurchase of their own shares, which increase EPS.

STOCK-MARKET-INDEX YIELD RATIO

This measure gets a little messy, but is meaningful in comparing bond and equity returns. It is calculated by dividing the 30-year, or long,

T-bond yield by the stock-market earnings yield. For instance, if the long T-bond yield is 6.00% and the S&P 500 earnings yield is 4.00%, the yield ratio is 1.5 (.06/.04 = 1.5). Since bonds have lower risk, you might expect the yield ratio to be closer to 1.0 or less. A high yield ratio suggests equities are relatively dear or, alternatively, bonds are relatively cheap. There is no clear, correct answer. It is simply another way to compare the relative valuation of stocks and bonds over time.

SUMMARY OF ECONOMIC AND MARKET STATISTICS

These data, taken as a whole, can help you stay abreast of broad conditions and trends in national economies and markets. They also can help you better understand the reports and comments your investment adviser directs to you. However, they merely provide the backdrop against which the real action, security analysis and selection, is played out.

11

SECURITY ANALYSIS

Security analysis is the combination of art and science that active money managers see as their craft. It consists of estimating a security's return and risk and comparing it with alternative investment opportunities. Its objective is to decide whether to buy, sell or hold that security in a portfolio. The initial step in security analysis is research, which can be divided into two broad categories. The first is **top-down**, which is based on a macroeconomic and political view of investment alternatives. For instance, if the U.S. Congress decided to extend the sales-tax moratorium on all Internet commerce, top-down investors would attempt to identify those industries and businesses that would be the financial winners and losers. An Internet bookseller like Amazon.com might be a winner, whereas a competitor selling primarily from superstores like the Borders Group might be a loser. The second category of research is **bottom-up**, which is based on a business-by-business evaluation of investment alternatives. An investor might read annual reports and meet with a company's management, customers and even competitors to assess its prospects of becoming a winner or loser. For instance, meeting with the management of Wal-Mart

Stores might convince you not only that it might be a winner, but also that a competitor like Kmart might be a loser.

The purpose of both categories of research is to winnow from the thousands of securities in the investing universe a manageable number, or shortlist, of candidates that merit the time and effort to analyze. The winnowing process is accomplished by screening. Investors screen for features that they regard as key determinants of security valuation. This is no small task and bears some resemblance to looking for needles in a haystack or panning for gold. Thankfully, computers and analytical databases of securities and their features make the investor's job much more efficient.

You also can find promising shortlist candidates by simply keeping your eyes and ears open. If you encounter a new business concept or uncommonly popular product with national sales potential in your daily life or travels, it might be worth closer scrutiny. A friend of mine in Sacramento is a motorcycle buff who is enamored of Harley-Davidson. During a recent visit, he suggested I take a look at the stock. New and innovative management has kick-started this manufacturer into a real winner despite the ubiquity of Japanese imports. Harley-Davidson has grown annual earnings at 42% for the five years ended March 31, 1998, and it shows in the stock price.

Once the shortlist of, say, one hundred securities is identified by screening, the real fun begins. Security analysis for debts is focused heavily on credit quality, yield and duration. It is less critical to become intimately familiar with the business of the issuer because you are not an owner. Security analysis for equities is generally divided into two broad styles.

TECHNICAL INDICATORS

The first style of equity analysis is **technical**, which primarily looks at market-price behavior. It is a number cruncher's dream come true. Technical investors who scour price charts attempting to discern levels of resistance and support for stocks are called **chartists**. They claim to see certain patterns in plots of stock prices like "head-and-shoulder formations," "flags" and "pennants." You might find technical analysis reminiscent of monkeys sitting in a tree trading bananas. It sure seems hard to see how all these extrinsic data can lead to sound conclusions about the underlying businesses. Nevertheless, its proponents swear it works for them. Like art, the beauty of market data is in the eye of the beholder. Technical investors also look to other market data that are extrinsic to the underlying security. These include the following.

DAILY VOLUME

This is the number of shares in any company traded on a given day. It can be related to the average daily number traded in, say, the last 30 days to discern rising or falling volume trends.

INSTITUTIONAL OWNERSHIP

This is available from the SEC and reveals how many of a company's shares are owned by institutions versus individuals. In 1998, it is estimated that institutions own about 50% of all outstanding U.S. equities. Since institutions can and do own large blocks of a single company, their trades can really move the price of smaller issues.

INSIDER TRADING

This is available from the SEC as well and reveals the trading activities of a company's owners who are connected to the business such as top managers and directors. If they are selling, or **bearish**, technical analysis suggests the shares are overvalued. If they are buying, or **bullish**, technical analysis suggests the shares are undervalued.

SHORT INTEREST

This is available from the various stock exchanges and reveals the number of a company's shares that have been sold short. Large short positions in a company are viewed by technical analysts as bearish. The short-interest ratio is a refinement of this measure. It shows the number of days required to equal the short interest if trading continued at the average daily volume for the month. For instance, on February 23, 1996, Chock Full O' Nuts, the coffee and tea processor, had a short-interest ratio of 45. It seems the stock's followers were chock full o' pessimism.

STOCK SPLITS

Economically, stock splits are a nonevent. If a company splits its stock two for one, the same shareholders have the same ownership claim before and after the split; they just have twice as many shares each of which is worth half as much. Just as in mathematics, the whole is not less than the sum of its parts. Nevertheless, companies continue to split their shares in the belief that a lower share price will attract more investors, call attention to the stock, and be perceived as a benefit to investors. Go figure! It sure defeats me.

EARNINGS SURPRISES

Most larger companies are tracked by one or more sell-side Wall Street analysts who predict quarterly earnings. These predictions are tallied regularly by firms like First Call and compared to the earnings actually reported by the company. If the company beats the consensus prediction, it is considered a positive earnings surprise. If the company falls short of the consensus prediction, it is considered a negative earnings surprise. Technical analysts believe that a positive earnings surprise can lift the demand for a company's stock almost instantaneously. They also believe that a negative earnings surprise has the opposite effect. There is a good deal of evidence that this is especially true at high stock-market yield ratios, since expected future earnings growth is the *sine qua non* of such lofty valuations.

INITIAL PUBLIC OFFERINGS

An initial public offering (IPO) is a company's debut in the public capital markets. Speculators and technically oriented investors snap them up in the hope that they will trade up in value immediately due in part to their newness. The facts suggest otherwise. Recently, there have been some spectacular examples of IPOs—especially Internet-driven businesses—that have soared through the roof like eBay, Inc. and MindSpring Enterprises. However, on average, IPOs underperform their relevant indices according to a number of recent studies. Additionally, not all new companies are destined to succeed as we discovered in examining the rule of 3s.

The sensible approach to evaluating IPOs is to read carefully the company's prospectus and focus on businesses that have experienced management and leadership positions in their industry. Since IPOs are often newly founded businesses, it can be very difficult to perform fundamental analysis due to their lack of operating history.

FUNDAMENTAL INDICATORS

The second style of equity analysis is **fundamental**. Fundamental investors favor either growth or value stocks and study a company's intrinsic features like sales, earnings, management, technical innovation and competitive environment, looking for reasons its stock might rise or fall. They compute all sorts of neat ratios from the financial statements and learn as much as they can about the company itself and its industry.

Growth

Growth investors look for bargains in companies with expanding sales and earnings. Typically, growth investors expect little or no cash dividends because the funds are needed internally to finance the rapid expansion of the business. Their focus includes the following measures.

PHYSICAL GROWTH RATE

The physical, or unit, growth rate is indicative of increasing customer acceptance without the need to adjust for inflation or company pricing policy. It might be measured in automobiles shipped or subscribers added. For example, MindSpring Enterprises, a micro-cap Internet access provider in Atlanta, saw its subscribership rise from 153,000 to 341,000 during the 12 months ended March 31, 1998, a physical growth rate of 123% [(341,000 - 153,000)/153,000 = 1.23].

REVENUE GROWTH RATE

The revenue, or dollar-sales, growth rate is indicative of management's ability to increase sales dollars. This can be done by raising prices, increasing physical volume, or rolling out new products and services.

Revenue growth rates also permit you to compare companies within an industry and draw conclusions about their market positions now and in the future.

EPS GROWTH RATE

The EPS growth rate of a company indicates how rapidly its annual earnings per share are increasing. It is another indicator of management's ability to improve profitability through either higher sales dollars and/or lower costs.

PEG RATIO

The annual EPS growth rate often is compared to the company's P/E ratio. This comparative indicator is called the P/E-to-growth (PEG) ratio. It is calculated by dividing the P/E ratio by the annual earnings growth rate. For instance, at March 31, 1998, Nautica Enterprises, the sportswear manufacturer, had a P/E of 23 and a trailing five-year EPS growth rate of 33%. Nautica's PEG ratio was .70 (23/33 = .70).

Growth investors like companies with PEG ratios of less than 1.0 and consider them potentially undervalued. Companies with PEG ratios well above 1.0 generally are considered pricey and must have other compelling features to be valued fairly. For instance, at March 31, 1998, Home Depot and Wal-Mart Stores had PEG ratios of 1.9 and 3.0, respectively. These seem astronomical, but their status as dominant players, or **category killers**, in their respective industries offers compelling additional value to investors.

Value

Value investors look for bargains in companies that have a margin of safety in their market price. Among other things, the margin of safety can stem from either a current valuation below the intrinsic worth of the business or future dividend growth. This often is called the "Graham and Dodd" approach because of their seminal book, *Security Analysis* (McGraw-Hill, 1934), the first edition of which appeared over sixty years ago. If the analytical side of investing floats your boat, as it does mine, I know of no better book anywhere.

Determining the margin of safety, or undervaluation, of a security is where the rubber meets the road. Value investors rely on a host of measures and ratios, many of which we covered in the section on accounting. The following discussion, which is by no means exhaustive, includes a few new ones.

Free Cash Flow

Free cash flow, or earnings before interest, taxes, depreciation and amortization (EBITDA) minus the capital expenditures necessary to grow the business, is considered one of the best indicators of a business' value. Cash, not accounting earnings, is what keeps a business **solvent** and able to grow without borrowing or issuing more shares. A company's free cash flow has to be mined from the financial statements and interviews with management, which requires considerable effort on the investor's part. The price-to-free cash flow (P/C) ratio of a business tells you how the stock is priced relative to the business' free cash flow per share. It is useful in comparing companies within and among industries.

Price-to-sales Ratio

The price-to-sales ratio (PSR) is computed by dividing a company's stock price by its annual sales per share. It reveals how many dollars you are paying for each dollar of annual sales. Take a look at Table 11-1, which presents three companies with vastly different PSRs on February 27, 1998.

If you wanted to own Pfizer, you had to pay $8.90 for each dollar of 1997 sales. That is a tidy sum and reflects not only the sales growth rate and profitability of the business, but also the impact on sales of Viagra, the nifty new potion, which promises to straighten everything short of the Leaning Tower of Pisa by merely ingesting a pill. Is this a great country or what? Apple Computer, on the other hand, looks like a real bargain at 46 cents for each dollar of 1997 sales. If Steven Jobs, the cofounder and recently appointed and anointed chief executive officer (CEO), can rekindle the magic that took this business from a California garage to Wall Street, 46 cents might be a real steal.

Table 11-1 PSRs

($ Rounded)

Company	Industry	02/27/98 Share Price	1997 Sales per Share	02/27/98 PSR
Pfizer	Health care	89	10	8.90
Maytag	Appliances	45	36	1.25
Apple	Computers	24	52	0.46

There is no correct PSR. Not surprisingly, value investors are inclined to pay far less than growth investors for $1.00 in annual sales. A company's PSR also provides a basis for comparison within and among industries that is less subject to fudging than EPS. The generally accepted accounting principles (GAAP) that govern the reporting of sales offer some choices, but nothing close to the number of choices available to the entire income statement. It might help you to think of each dollar of sales as an opportunity to make either a profit or loss. A business' quality of management and competitive environment determines which it will be.

DIVIDEND GROWTH RATE

Value stocks can be surprisingly good income producers. This is a component of their margin of safety and helps buoy their value in down markets. Just as importantly, value stocks frequently increase their dividend payments over time, which makes them even more attractive. Let's take a look at bonds versus value stocks in this regard. If you buy $100,000 of 20-year T-bonds at face value with a coupon of 5.8%, you are entitled to $5,800 (100,000 x .058 = 5,800) per year for the next 20 years. At maturity, your $100,000 will be returned. Alternatively, if you buy $100,000 of, say, the common stock of Dow Chemical, the large-cap chemical and materials producer, which presently yields 3.6%, has a PSR of 1.04 and a P/E of 12, your expected annual income the first year is $3,600 (100,000 x .036 = 3,600). If Dow Chemical's board of directors votes to increase the cash dividend at the annual rate of, say, 6%, the annual income on your $100,000 investment will double about every 12 years according to the rule of 72. Let's compare this over the life of the bond in Table 11-2.

Table 11-2   Dividend Growth
                                   versus T-bond
                                 $100,000 Invested

Year	T-bond Income		Dow Chemical Dividend
1	$ 5,800		$ 3,600
2	5,800		3,816
3	5,800		4,045
4	5,800		4,288
5	5,800		4,545
6	5,800		4,818
7	5,800		5,107
8	5,800		5,413
9	5,800	*Yields are equal*	5,738
10	5,800		6,082
11	5,800		6,447
12	5,800		6,834
13	5,800	*Dividend doubles*	7,244
14	5,800		7,679
15	5,800		8,139
16	5,800		8,628
17	5,800		9,145
18	5,800		9,694
19	5,800		10,276
20	5,800		10,892
Total	$116,000		$132,430

As you can see, the yields approach equality in the ninth year of ownership. After the tenth year, the Dow Chemical annual dividend exceeds the T-bond yield in dollars. After 20 years, you have collected $16,430 (132,430 - 116,000 = 16,430), or 14%, more in dividends than T-bond interest before adjusting for the time value of the payments and income taxes. More importantly, 20 years from now you stand a very good chance of receiving more than the original $100,000 investment from the Dow Chemical stock. Without counting dividends, it has grown in price about 14% annually for the five years ending March 31, 1998. At half that rate, or 7%, in 20 years your Dow Chemical stock would be worth $386,968 [(100,000) x (1.07)^20 = 386,968] before capital-gains tax of 20%. After capital-gains tax of $57,394 [(386,968 - 100,000) x .20 = 57,394], your stock would be worth $329,574 (386,968 - 57,394 = 329,574). In contrast, at maturity, your 20-year T-bonds would be redeemed unceremoniously at their face value of $100,000 with no taxes due.

Is this a no-brainer or what? These value investors have sure got this right. Of course, we know there is no guarantee that Dow Chemical stock will rise annually in value by 7%—or by any amount for that matter—but if you spread your $100,000 across 10 or 15 high-yielding stocks instead of just Dow Chemical, your chances of accomplishing the same result with far less unsystematic risk are greatly improved. Another approach to the same objective is a value-oriented or utility-stock mutual fund that yields well above the S&P 500 index. Value stocks with steadily increasing dividends can let you have your cake and eat it too. They are especially effective in retirement accounts where current income eventually may become important.

Stock Buybacks

Stock buybacks attract value investors because, unlike purely cosmetic stock splits, they are economic events. Imagine a company's board of directors sitting around a polished mahogany table of regal dimensions and grandeur discussing how to deal with a cash balance that vastly exceeds its needs for both liquidity and the capital expenditures necessary to grow the business. They can vote to embark on an acquisition binge, sit on the funds and earn money-market interest rates, pay the CEO and his minions a huge bonus, declare a large, taxable dividend to shareholders, or buy back their own shares in the secondary market. Provided the stock is not selling above intrinsic value, value investors find the buyback of shares by far the most palatable choice. Buybacks exchange company cash that can earn, say, 4.5% in short-term, liquid investments for its own shares, which are presumably capable of handily outperforming cash. Additionally, buybacks often are accompanied by dividend increases.

Let's look at how the numbers work. IBM announced on April 28, 1998 that it would buy back $3.5 billion of its some 972 million common shares. The shares are trading at about $115 with a P/E of 19, so this amounts to about 30 million shares, or about 3% (30 million/972 million = .0309), of total outstanding shares. IBM also announced it would boost the quarterly dividend by 10% from 20 cents to 22 cents. Before the buyback, each common share of IBM was entitled to its 1997 EPS of $6.01 and its annual cash dividend of 80 cents. After the buyback, each common share is entitled to 1997 EPS of $6.20 (6.01/(1.00 - .03) = 6.20) and its increased annual dividend of 88 cents. At a P/E of 19, each share is revalued at $118 (6.20 x 19 = 118). For the tidy-minded among you, I have ignored the slight reduction in EPS attributable to the loss of interest income on the $3.5 billion. It amounts to about 12 cents per share after taxes [(3.5 billion x .045 x .7)/942 million = .12]. Whew! That was a bunch of numbers, so let's summarize in Table 11-3.

Table 11-3

Stock Buyback
IBM @ $115
At: 04/28/98

Per Share	Before Buyback	After Buyback	$ Benefit	% Benefit
Price	$115.00	$118.00	$3.00	
Annual dividend	0.80	0.88	0.08	
Value: 1st year	$115.80	$118.88	$3.08	2.66%

In one fell swoop, IBM has increased the first-year value of each share by almost 2.7%. The bulk of this increase is share price, which is not subject to tax unless the share is sold. This result is called **anti-dilutive**. For the investors who remain owners, it effectively divides the very same pie, IBM's future earnings, into slices that are larger than before. When compounding over time is applied to both the increased share price and dividend, it becomes even more rewarding to investors. Incidentally, value investors are justifiably unimpressed with buybacks that are used to satisfy employee stock-option plans or to fund acquisition programs. As soon as the stock returns to the secondary market, the benefit of the buyback is history.

PRICE-TO-BOOK VALUE

This measure reveals the ratio of a company's share price to its total assets less liabilities, or book value, per share. For example, a company trading at $30.00 per share with a book value per share of $15.00 has a price-to-book value ratio of 2.00 (30.00/15.00 = 2.00). Historically, value investors have focused more on balance sheet analysis and have placed great weight on how cheaply they could purchase a company's book value. This was far more relevant in years past when most major U.S. companies were engaged in businesses that had large balances in their property, plant and equipment accounts like manufacturers and railroads. As we discovered in the section on accounting, the most important assets of many modern companies are not reflected adequately—or at all—in their balance sheets. For instance, Intel's engineering expertise and Coca-Cola's marketing clout are conspicuously absent except in their exceptional sales and earnings figures. Consequently, price-to-book value ratios are practically obsolete except for businesses whose balance sheets contain mostly monetary assets and liabilities, such as banks and other financial-service providers.

Universal

There are some indicators of corporate valuation that apply to both growth and value stocks. These include the following.

ECONOMIC VALUE ADDED

Investors long have recognized that accounting information based on GAAP is not the sharpest knife in the drawer when it comes to analyzing wealth creation by a business. A growing number of both CEOs and investment analysts look to economic value added (EVA) for this purpose. Although EVA flows logically from traditional microeconomic analysis,

Stern Stewart & Co., a leading consulting firm, has advanced its application to modern business enterprises and registered the related trademark.

In its simplest form, EVA is a business' net operating profit after taxes less the after-tax cost of capital (both debt and equity). The proponents of EVA correctly point out that earnings computed in accordance with GAAP recognize the cost of interest on debt, but conspicuously fail to recognize the cost of equity capital. In effect, they are saying that the GAAP-based income statement of a business does not reflect the economic substance of its results of operations. Despite my instinctive desire to reject this iconoclastic notion and to rush to the defense of my fellow CPAs, I must agree that EVA provides an elegant and understandable framework for financial decision making and analysis. It can be particularly useful in educating and incentivizing the nonfinancial members of an organization, which is borne out by numerous corporate success stories including Coca-Cola, Eli Lilly and SPX.

The calculation of EVA requires some data mining and adjusting of traditional accounting information, but the calculus is straightforward and the results can be remarkable. The latter is especially true when EVA improvements form the basis for incentive-compensation schemes, which result in far greater alignment of the economic interests of the employees and shareholders of a business—the ultimate form of eating your own cooking.

MARKET VALUE ADDED

Another analytical tool that flows from the EVA approach is market value added (MVA). Simply put, MVA is the value reflected in the stock market of a business less the adjusted book value of its capital (both debt and equity). Because in most industries GAAP mandates the writing off of certain economically significant assets like **research and development (R&D)** and goodwill, they must be added back to equity capital in computing MVA.

MVA reveals how effectively management has performed its job as steward of the capital invested in a business. If MVA is positive, management has created value; if MVA is negative, management has destroyed value. Approximations of MVA based on unadjusted total capital for three companies at the date of their most recent annual reports is shown in Table 11-4.

Table 11-4   MVA
                                          ($ Millions)

Company	Latest Annual Report	MV Approx. Market Value	D Unadj. Debt Capital	E Unadj. Equity Capital	MV - (D + E) = MVA + or (-)
Harnischfeger	10/31/98	364	963	667	(1,266)
Kmart	01/28/98	8,565	1,725	5,643	1,197
Wal-Mart	01/31/98	198,582	7,191	18,503	172,888

As you can see, Wal-Mart has created MVA of nearly $173 billion, or 6.7 times $(172{,}888/(7{,}191 + 18{,}503) = 6.73)$, its unadjusted total capital. Kmart, on the other hand, has created MVA of $1.2 billion, or 0.16 times $(1{,}197/(1{,}725 + 5{,}643) = .162)$, its unadjusted total capital. You are free to draw your own conclusions about which of these broadline retailers has more effective management. Unhappily, MVA also can be destroyed. Harnischfeger Industries has destroyed MVA of almost $1.3 billion, or -0.78 times $(-1{,}266/(963 + 667) = -.777)$, its unadjusted total capital. According to the notes to its latest audited financial statements, this is assignable in part to the recent, precipitous economic decline in Asia. It also reflects a management decision—presumably ratified by its board of directors during a less-than-lucid interval—to assume a mammoth credit risk from an Indonesian paper-mill customer of Beloit Corporation, a majority-owned subsidiary, which, sadly, may prove enormously costly.

MVA provides a powerful tool for judging on a common basis the valuation of dissimilar businesses. MVA's elegance lies in the fact that the unique risk characteristics of a business are already baked into its stock-market value, which represents the collective judgment of investors. If your appetite for this subject remains unsatisfied, I recommend reading *EVA: The Real Key to Creating Wealth* (John Wiley & Sons, 1998) by Al Ehrbar. It is peppered with anecdotes and an excellent read for anyone who is interested in a practical approach to understanding and improving the value of a business.

SUMMARY OF SECURITY ANALYSIS

The lion's share of security analysis is performed and disseminated by analysts who work for sell-side Wall Street firms. There are some very talented people among them, but the inherent conflict of interest their firms face is unavoidable. Some insiders have observed sagely that the term "independent Wall Street research" is oxymoronic. On the one hand, these firms offer to take companies public for a princely fee and follow them with ratings and research reports; on the other hand, they hold out their analysts to the investing public as objective stock pickers whose buy and sell ratings are their bond. But if a firm's analyst pans the stock of a company it took public, it has a chilling effect on future business with that issuer. On second thought, *arctic* might be a better choice than chilling. The net effect of this conflict can be less-than-impartial advice, which is detrimental to investors and advisers who rely on the research reports. This can apply equally to IPOs and stocks traded in the secondary market. The only way I know to guard against this bias is to place greater weight on the research produced by sell-side firms who neither work nor act as a market maker for the issuer in question. Recent academic studies of IPOs suggest this approach is more reliable. It often is possible to ascertain the relationship between the analyst's firm and the issuer by speaking to the firm's management or the shareholder-relations department of the issuer.

Finally, there are a large number of smaller and neglected stocks that no analysts regularly follow. They sometimes are called **shadow stocks** because they exist outside the purview of Wall Street. Shadow stocks can be a fertile vineyard in which to toil for investors who are prepared to do their own analysis. Since information is limited, their chances are greater of discovering margins of safety in the pricing of shadow stocks. This can be rewarding for patient investors if the intrinsic value of these stocks gains wider recognition by the market.

12

PERFORMANCE MEASUREMENT

Performance measurement can be summed up in two basic questions:

1. How'ya doin'?
2. Compared to what?

Despite their colloquial plainness, these are exactly the right questions to ask. Surprisingly, most investors are unable to answer them because precious few brokerage firms, trust departments and financial planners calculate meaningful performance data for their clients. As a result, a growing number of consultants, independent accounting firms, and investor-arbitration experts offer this service for a fee to investors. The time to discuss performance reporting is when you are opening or moving your accounts. If a prospective adviser doesn't provide this service on a personalized basis, you should be prepared to either hire an independent person to provide it or at least review it yourself. Even if a prospective adviser does provide personalized performance reporting, you should possess enough knowledge to evaluate the reports. It's your money and you have an obligation to yourself to monitor periodically results and hold accountable the professionals you hire.

Let's find the most effective way to answer our two basic questions. If you still have the armbands and green eyeshade handy, this would be a good time to put them on. We are going to delve into the numbers again, but as always I'll do my level best to exorcise the demon of complexity.

HOW'YA DOIN'?

Performance measurement presents a number of considerations. Let's take a look at each of them.

TOTAL RETURN

Total return for a stated period is the sum of security-price changes and income. Total return applies equally to all investments including debts and equities. In the case of debts, total return is principal change plus interest. In the case of equities, total return is stock-price change plus dividends, if any, which can consist of either cash or stock. Table 12-1 contains the necessary elements to calculate the total return of PachydermWorks, a large-cap growth stock, for the four quarters ended December 31, 1998.

The total return of PachydermWorks' stock for the first quarter ended March 31, 1998 is 33%. This percentage is arrived at by the shortcut formula: $[((EP + I)/BP) - 1] \times 100 = $ Total return %, where "EP" is ending share price, "I" is income and "BP" is beginning share price. I have keyed this formula into a spreadsheet, which lets me perform these calculations on my PC. Let's run the formula: $[((64 + 0)/48) - 1] \times 100 = 33.33$, or 33%. This is a hefty return for one quarter, but remember that PachydermWorks just rolled out the spousal-prevarication analyzer and is a darling of Wall Street analysts. Happily, total return agrees with the table for the first quarter. Now, let's run it for the second quarter ending June 30, 1998, during which PachydermWorks' shares declined in value by $6.00: $[((58 + 0)/64) - 1] \times 100 = -9.38$, or -9%. *Voila!* We again have agreement with the table. Despite its promising new analyzer, PachydermWorks may have reported less-than-anticipated EPS for the first quarter, which resulted in the stock price falling.

Table 12-1
Total Return
PachydermWorks
(Rounded)

	1st Quarter 03/31/98	2nd Quarter 06/30/98	3rd Quarter 09/30/98	4th Quarter 12/31/98
Beg. share price	$48	$64	$58	$60
Dividends				
End share price	$64	$58	$60	$56
Return + or (-):				
Share price	$16	($6)	$2	($4)
Dividends				
Total return:				
$	$16	($6)	$2	($4)
%	33%	(9%)	3%	(7%)

ANNUAL COMPOUND TOTAL RETURN

Performance figures for security prices and indices can be based on price changes alone or total return. For example, the version of the Dow Jones industrial average (DJIA) that is so often the focus of the media is based on the daily price changes of its 30 component stocks. In contrast, annual compound total return indices combine price changes and the assumed reinvestment on the pay date of all income into additional securities of the issuer at that day's price. Provided the issuer or index in question pays income, annual compound total return is, of course, always higher. The 1998 annual compound total return for PachydermWorks, which pays no dividend, is 17% using the shortcut formula: $[((EP + I)/BP) - 1] \times 100$ = Total return %. Let's run the numbers: $[((56 + 0)/48) - 1] \times 100 =$ 16.67, or 17%.

Notice that 17% is less than the sum of the four quarterly returns. This is due to the power of compounding, which you first encountered in the section on compound interest. This is very important to see, so please refer again to Table 12-1. The four quarterly returns are 33%, -9%, 3% and -7%. Simply adding them results in 20%. Here is where it really gets exciting! The annual compound total return is computed by adding one to each decimal quarterly return, multiplying the sums times each other in sequence, subtracting one from that result, and converting to a percentage. Let's give it a try: $[((1 + .33) \times (1 - .09) \times (1 + .03) \times (1 - .07)) -1] \times 100$ = 15.93, or 16%. Math mavens call this geometric linking. As you can see, the geometrically linked, or compound, result is very close to 16.67, or 17%, which was computed using the shortcut formula.

Additions/Withdrawals

Both the shortcut and quarterly compound formulae we just used work acceptably if there are no significant additions or withdrawals during the measured period. In either of these events, adjustments must be made in the calculations to avoid mixing apples and oranges in the total return. Let's consider what happens in the event of an addition. Suppose you open an account with Avarice & Cupidity Investment Counsel on January 1, 1998, purchase 1,000 shares of PachydermWorks at $48 and hold it for a year. Further, suppose that your cruel but fair boss awards you a performance bonus of $12,000 on December 1, 1998 with which you promptly purchase, based on sell-side analysts' recommendations, an additional 200 shares of your favorite company PachydermWorks and add it to your account. Lastly, suppose that Avarice & Cupidity Investment Counsel contract to manage your account for 100 basis points, or 1%, for the first year payable at year-end.

On January 1, 1999, you call Mr. Elbert Avarice and request a performance report on your account for the year ended December 31, 1998. He promptly returns your call and reports that your account, compounded quarterly, has returned an enviable 40% **gross of fees**, or 39% **net of fees**, and handily beat the S&P 500 total return index for the year. You register surprise and ask him to fax the calculation and an account summary. They are presented on the following page and in Table 12-2.

1. Total return calculation: $[((1 + .33) \times (1 - .09) \times (1 + .03) \times (1 + .12)) - 1] \times 100 = 39.6$, or 40%
2. Account summary:

Table 12-2

Total Return
Your a/c
Year: '98
(Rounded)

	1st Quarter 03/31/98	2nd Quarter 06/30/98	3rd Quarter 09/30/98	4th Quarter 12/31/98
Beg. price	$48	$64	$58	$60
Beg. a/c	$48,000	$64,000	$58,000	$60,000
Dividends				
Contributions/				$12,000
(Withdrawals)				
End price	$64	$58	$60	$56
End a/c	$64,000	$58,000	$60,000	$67,200
Return + or (-):				
Share price	$16,000	($6,000)	$2,000	$7,200
Dividends				
Total return:				
$	$16,000	($6,000)	$2,000	$7,200
%	33%	(9%)	3%	12%

Before reviewing the calculations, you run the shortcut formula to double-check the results. It looks like this: $[((EP + I)/BP) - 1] \times 100 =$ Total return %. So, $[((67,200 + 0)/48,000) - 1] \times 100 = 40.00$, or 40%. It looks to you like Elbert got it right after all, but something gnaws at you. Upon examining the account summary, you zero in on the treatment of the

$12,000 bonus. It ended up in the year-end account balance, but is not included in the beginning account balance. Surely, Avarice & Cupidity shouldn't get credit in their performance figures for a contribution. After discussing your doubts with I.M. Partial & Co., an independent CPA firm, you are advised that contributions and withdrawals must be neutralized in computing investment returns. You are advised further that failing to properly treat contributions got the Beardstown Ladies into a real pickle with performance reporting and caused them to hire Price Waterhouse to fix the numbers. Sadly, the audited results were not nearly as good as their delightful recipes.

Armed with this knowledge, you then recompute the quarterly returns with the following formula: $[((EV - NA)/BV) - 1] \times 100 =$ Quarterly return %, where "EV" is the ending account value, "NA" is the net additions to the account and "BV" is the beginning account value. This produces the result shown in Table 12-3.

Table 12-3

Quarterly Returns
Your a/c
Year: '98
(Rounded)

	1st Quarter 03/31/98	2nd Quarter 06/30/98	3rd Quarter 09/30/98	4th Quarter 12/31/98
BV	$48,000	$64,000	$58,000	$60,000
NA				$12,000
EV	$64,000	$58,000	$60,000	$67,200
Total return:				
$	$16,000	($6,000)	$2,000	($4,800)
%	33%	(9%)	3%	(8%)

Next, you link these quarterly returns and compute the annual compound total return as follows: $[((1 + .33) \times (1 - .09) \times (1 + .03) \times (1$

- .08)) - 1] x 100 = 14.69, or 15%. Color you mad! You call Elbert Avarice and inform him that the correct performance figure for 1998 is 15% gross of fees, or 14% net of fees, which is well below the index. You further inform him that effective immediately you have decided to close your account and invest $15,000 per quarter in a diversified open-end mutual fund which specializes in small-cap growth stocks. It is called MicroMidas Growth Fund.

TIME-WEIGHTED VERSUS DOLLAR-WEIGHTED RETURN

Avarice & Cupidity drag their feet in closing your account and finally send a check on March 15, 1999. You decide to increase your quarterly contributions to $20,000 beginning April 1, 1999 to make up for lost time. Table 12-4 reflects your investment program in MicroMidas for 1999.

You dutifully compute the quarterly compound returns for your investment in MicroMidas using the formula: [((EV - NA)/BV) - 1] x 100 = Quarterly return %. At year-end, you compound the quarterly returns and come up with -14% as follows: [((1 + .20) x (1 - .23) x (1 -.07)) - 1] x 100 = -14.07, or -14%. You are not a happy camper! The very next day you receive a shareholder's letter from MicroMidas Growth Fund, which describes in nautical terms how the eminently able and intrepid manager captained the fund through the perilous reefs and shoals of investing and produced a creditable time-weighted return of 32% gross of fees for the year ended December 31, 1999. The performance chart in Table 12-5 is included for your perusal.

The moment your shock wears off, you grab your trusty calculator and geometrically link the returns in the report as follows: [((1 + .33) x (1 + .20) x (1 - .13) x (1 - .05)) - 1] x 100 = 31.91, or 32%. What's wrong with this picture? How can MicroMidas report a handsome gain when you are painfully aware of the loss you have suffered? Resignedly, you vow to redouble your efforts to encourage any children and grandchildren you might have to take as many math courses as they possibly can.

A call to I.M. Partial & Co. clears things up in a big hurry. Isabella Partial, CPA/PFS, patiently explains that mutual funds always report their results using time-weighted returns. The time-weighted return of 32% reflects the results you would have experienced if you had put in $1.00 at

Table 12-4   Performance Measurement
MicroMidas
Year: '99
(Rounded)

	1st Quarter 03/31/99	2nd Quarter 06/30/99	3rd Quarter 09/30/99	4th Quarter 12/31/99
Beg. price	$15	$20	$24	$21
Beg. shares		1,000	1,000	1,833
Beg. a/c		$20,000	$24,000	$38,493
Contributions			$20,000	$20,000
Shares bought			833	952
End price	$20	$24	$21	$20
End shares		1,000	1,833	2,785
End a/c		$24,000	$38,493	$55,700
BV		$20,000	$24,000	$38,493
NA			$20,000	$20,000
EV		$24,000	$38,493	$55,700
Total return:				
$	n/a	$4,000	($5,507)	($2,793)
%	n/a	20%	(23%)	(7%)

the beginning of the year and kept it invested until year-end. It highlights the skill, or lack thereof, of the fund manager. She calls it the **fund return**. Unfortunately, you chose to begin investing quarterly on April 1, 1999 and did not experience the 32% gain chalked up by the fund for the year. You experienced a dollar-weighted return of -14%. She calls it the **shareholder return**.

Table 12-5   Performance
                              MicroMidas
                              Year: '99
                              (Rounded)

	1st Quarter 03/31/99	2nd Quarter 06/30/99	3rd Quarter 09/30/99	4th Quarter 12/31/99	Compound Annual
Beg. price	$15	$20	$24	$21	$15
End price	$20	$24	$21	$20	$20
Total return:					
$	$5	$4	($3)	($1)	$5
%	33%	20%	(13%)	(5%)	32%

An analogy that helps me keep these returns in perspective is travel by train. Let's say a train leaves weekly from Grand Central Station in New York City bound for Seattle, the city of utopian investment returns, with intermediate stops in Chicago, Minneapolis and Boise. The entire trip, which consists of four legs, is scheduled to take 48 hours. I promise this isn't one of those "when will the trains collide" problems, so please keep reading! Further, let's say that the train arrives timely in Chicago and you board with a ticket to Boise. After arriving an hour late in Minneapolis, the train encounters a herd of American bison, which has strayed from one of Ted Turner's many ranches, and pulls into Boise three hours late. Your aunt Minnie, who has been patiently awaiting your arrival with a fruit pie that she baked for you that very day, is as annoyed as you are. Your impression of the railroad company's performance is negative since they blew the schedule and caused you to arrive late. The train then proceeds to Seattle at record speed and makes up all the lost time. The folks who boarded in New York City bound for Seattle disembark fully satisfied with the railroad company's performance. After all, they arrived on time and were even treated to a close look at that thundering herd of buffalo.

The performance of the railroad company for the entire trip is akin to the time-weighted, or fund, return. It reflects the experience of a passenger who boarded in New York City and remained on the train to its final destination. The performance of the railroad company for your two legs of the trip, from Chicago to Minneapolis and onward to Boise, is akin to the dollar-weighted, or shareholder, return. It reflects the experience of a passenger who boarded in Chicago and only remained on the train to Boise. Paradoxically, each of these passengers ended up with a legitimately different impression about performance.

The point to all this is simple. Your actions as a shareholder influence how your investment performs. The fair way to measure the fund manager as an investor is time-weighted; the fair way to measure yourself as an investor is dollar-weighted.

CUMULATIVE RETURN

The promotional materials of mutual funds and investment advisers often contain nifty graphs and bar charts that show how much an initial investment, say, ten years ago would be worth today. They look mighty impressive and leave the distinct impression that investing is no more difficult than plucking low-hanging fruit in an orchard. These same promotional materials often cite the cumulative return from inception to date of newer funds. For instance, let's say the MicroMidas Growth Fund presents the bar chart shown in Figure 12-1.

The chart shows an initial investment of $10,000 in MicroMidas growing to $24,500 in the eight years ending December 31, 1998. In order to restate this in terms of an annual compound rate, which is far more familiar to most people, you have to do a little math. You can estimate the compound return by using the handy rule of 72. Let's first convert the 145% growth back to merely doubling, or 100%: (100/145 = .69). So, if the investment grew 145% in 8 years, it grew 100%, or about doubled, in 5.5 (.69 x 8 = 5.5) years. Now, if you divide the constant 72 by 5.5, the number of years to double, you arrive at the average annual compound return of 13.09% (72/5.5 = 13.09). That sure makes it easier to grasp how MicroMidas performed over the past eight years. Be aware that this is the fund's *average* compound return. You have no idea how much it varied from year to year; you also have no idea if it lost money in any one or more of the last eight years. Such are the limitations of averages.

Figure 12-1

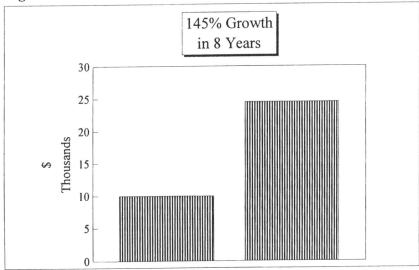

145% Growth
in 8 Years

Now that you have computed ably the approximate average compound total return of 13.09%, let's take a look at the more elegant formula that provides the precise answer. Remember the way you geometrically linked MicroMidas' quarterly returns earlier to compute the annual compound return? The formula you employed required adding one to each decimal quarterly return, multiplying the sums times each other in sequence, subtracting one from that result, and converting to a percentage. In that case, you knew the quarterly returns and simply applied the formula. In this case, you must solve for the average annual rate that, when geometrically linked for eight years, raises $10,000 to $24,500. By rearranging the formula, we derive the following: $10,000 x (1 + r)^8 = $24,500, where "r" is the average annual compound return and "^8" is the spreadsheet protocol for the eighth power. Here's where it gets a little tougher. After again rearranging the formula to solve for "r," it looks like this: r = (2.45^(1/8)) - 1, where "^(1/8)" is the spreadsheet protocol for the eighth root. Keying this into the spreadsheet produces 11.85%, which is not exactly the same as the 13.09% that the rule of 72 produced, but pretty close. This points up the fact that the rule of 72 is only an estimating technique. Its virtues are speed and simplicity. It also works best in return ranges at or below 12% due to its mathematical derivation as a constant.

That was a bunch of work, but, happily, we were able to convert the slick bar chart into something readily grasped, its average annual compound return. Being the astute investors we are, we also would ask if the return of 145% over eight years was gross or net of fees and if income was assumed to have been reinvested in the fund's shares, i.e., if total return was used.

FEES AND EXPENSES

Investment-management fees and expenses must be considered in evaluating investment returns. Debt owners are particularly sensitive to fees and expenses because their returns are typically slim. On the other hand, if the portfolio has performed well, equity owners tend to view fees and expenses as justified. If the portfolio has performed poorly, they are far less charitable in their thinking. The treatment of fees should be disclosed in any presentation of investment results. Naturally, results gross of fees are always higher than results net of fees.

INCOME TAXES

For taxable accounts, there is no thornier performance issue than income taxes. Typically, investment performance is presented before taxes. This practice stems in part from the historical dominance of institutional investors whose status was predominately tax-exempt. Unfortunately, it serves taxable accounts ill. Additionally, your tax bracket can change from year to year and, of course, tax brackets may differ significantly from one investor to the next. Instead of tackling this issue head-on, most investment advisers just punt and let you untangle the tax issues.

In making comparisons among available returns, debt owners must convert tax-exempt income to its taxable equivalent. This is relatively straightforward and was covered amply in the section on Munis. Equities, particularly equity mutual funds, are less clear. As we noted in the section on taxation, actively managed equity mutual funds potentially can generate significant capital gains in different tax brackets depending on the holding period. Additionally, a mutual fund may have embedded capital gains or losses in its asset base when you purchase its shares. These are called **unrealized**. If your account is taxable and the fund contains unrealized gains, you have paid full price for the fund's shares despite the eventual likelihood of a tax bill upon receipt of distributions from the fund. The extent to which a fund contains unrealized gains or losses is usually ascertainable by examining the financial statements and accompanying notes in its semiannual or annual report. For taxable accounts, both income and capital-gains taxes are important considerations in evaluating investment results.

CONSISTENT PERFORMANCE REPORTING

The foregoing examples point up the crying need for consistent and understandable performance presentation standards. They also reaffirm an old saw, which holds that "figures don't lie, but liars can figure." You are exposed to the whims of investment advisers if you request performance data in the absence of any standards. In effect, you are asking them to grade their own papers. Happily, in 1993, the Association for Investment Management and Research in Charlottesville, Virginia met this need with its **performance presentation standards (PPS)**. AIMR-PPS define the manner in which performance data must be presented and even require adherence to certain calculation standards such as time-weighting on at least a quarterly basis. AIMR-PPS have been adopted by most U.S. professional investment organizations and circulated internationally in an effort to derive a set of global standards. We need not immerse ourselves in the details of AIMR-PPS, but you ought to ensure that any investment adviser whom you hire adheres to them. Otherwise you really don't know what you're looking at when you read sales literature or investment results. At the risk of offending their readers, I doubt any of you ever would have heard of the Beardstown Ladies if they had complied with AIMR-PPS.

COMPARED TO WHAT?

Our second question deals with judging investment results once they are presented fairly. It also raises a number of considerations. Let's take a look at them.

PURCHASING POWER

At the very least, most investors seek to maintain the purchasing power of their assets. In recent years, this has been easy to do with equities, but not so easy with debts. Except for their inflation-adjusted brethren, debts have a fixed principal amount that is repaid at maturity. The only way you stand a chance of maintaining purchasing power with debts is to reinvest some or all of the interest payments in additional securities. If, in the presence of inflation, you spend all the interest currently, investment-grade debts are guaranteed to decline in purchasing power, or real terms, over the long haul. That is the reward you receive for assuming little or no risk.

Comparing the investment results of a diversified portfolio with the CPI is shown in Table 12-6. Two facts are immediately apparent. First, the account handily beat inflation by over 9%. Second, the income alone before fees amounted to 3% (1,200/40,000 = .03) of the beginning account value and was less than the year's inflation rate. This suggests that in a year when security prices are flat, the account may underperform inflation.

Table 12-6

Performance
Your a/c
Year: '00

Beg. account value	$40,000
Income	1,200
Fees & expenses	(600)
End account value	$45,000
Net total return:	
$	$5,000
%	12.50%
Inflation (CPI)	(3.25%)
Real return	9.25%

PEER-GROUP RANKINGS

Investors often find it useful to know where their mutual funds or investment managers stand in comparison to their peers. This is a lot like the rankings you receive in high school based on your grade point average in relation to the rest of your graduating class. I vaguely recall that mine was less than stellar, but, of course, my graduating class was uncommonly erudite, which softened the blow a little. In any case, that's my story and I'm sticking to it! For mutual funds, rankings are available from statistical-service providers like Lipper, Inc. and Morningstar, Inc. Lipper defines investment categories, assigns funds to them, and ranks them periodically by total return. Funds ranking in the top 20% are rated "A," funds ranking in the next 20% are rated "B," and so forth. On the other hand, Morningstar employs a star system that resembles the rating systems historically used for restaurants and hotels. Stars are awarded to a fund according to criteria developed by Morningstar; the more stars, the better the fund. Thankfully, Siskel and Ebert chose films instead of funds to rate, otherwise we would be confronted with thumbs as a rating system.

For investment managers, the peer groups and rankings typically are assembled by investment-consulting firms that provide these data to clients as part of their services. Peer-group rankings can be particularly useful in evaluating funds and managers when the investment style to which they are committed is temporarily out of favor. For instance, if a small-cap growth manager underperforms the **Russell 2000 index** by, say, 5%, but ranks in the top 20% of his or her peers, you may derive some consolation from this high ranking. At least this manager is among the best of the underperformers, which suggests that when his or her investment style returns to favor, this manager is more likely to produce good results than his or her peers.

BENCHMARKS

This term, which is borrowed from the surveyor's lexicon, covers the unmanaged indicators that are best suited to compare with investment results within asset classes. For instance, comparing PachydermWorks' performance with the S&P 500 would make good sense because it is a large-cap U.S. stock. Similarly, comparing MouseWorks' performance with the Russell 2000 would be logical since it is a micro-cap U.S. stock.

Benchmarks exist for all the major classes of debts and equities and are regularly published in the financial press. The best known for U.S. debts is the Lehman Brothers (LB) series, which covers taxable and tax-exempt debt instruments over all maturity ranges. The most familiar benchmarks for U.S. stocks are the Dow Jones industrial average (DJIA) and the Standard & Poor's (S&P) 500 index. The DJIA is weighted by price and includes only 30 representative issuers. The S&P 500 is weighted by market capitalization and includes primarily the 500 largest issuers. Despite its narrow coverage and weighting by price, many individual investors faithfully follow the DJIA. On the other hand, investment professionals are more inclined to follow the S&P 500 due to its broader coverage. Benchmarks also are produced for foreign stocks (the Morgan Stanley Capital International (MSCI) Europe, Australia and Far East (EAFE) index), socially responsible stocks (the Domini social index), and just about any other major asset class you can imagine. The key to benchmarking is to match your investments with the most relevant indicators.

In the case of diversified portfolios holding two or more asset classes, you easily can create a composite benchmark by weighting the asset classes in target annual percentages. Let's take a look at the example reflected in Table 12-7.

There are a number of points worthy of mention in this table. First of all, your account's return handily whipped inflation, our old nemesis. Despite its 12.50% total return net of fees for the year ended December 31, 2000, your portfolio underperformed its unmanaged composite index by 3.04% (15.54 - 12.50 = 3.04), or 304 basis points. This underperformance can be found mostly in your equity holdings, which lagged the S&P 500 index by 5.30% (22.00 - 16.70 = 5.30). Your bond holdings only lagged the LBI by .35% (5.85 - 5.50 = .35), or 35 basis points. Secondly, the composite index used as a benchmark for your account is based on weighting the LBI and the S&P 500 40% and 60%, respectively, since this is your target, or desired, asset allocation. The actual return for the year is based on the beginning allocation of 37.5% bonds and 62.5% stock. This allocation can change daily. It ended the year at 33.3% bonds and 66.7% stock. In order to restore the account to the target allocation percentages, you will have to rebalance by selling some stock holdings and adding the proceeds to bonds or allocating new cash to the account. The latter is preferable in taxable accounts, because no taxable events are triggered. Additionally, your account's return for the year does not take into account any income or capital-gains taxes that you may owe.

Table 12-7

Performance
Your a/c
Year: '00
(Rounded)

	Annual Return	12/31/00 Market Value	12/31/00 Allocation	Target Allocation
Fixed income:				
Bonds	5.50%	$15,000	33.3%	40.0%
LB index (LBI)	5.85%			
Equities:				
Large-cap stocks	16.70%	$30,000	66.7%	60.0%
S&P 500 index	22.00%			
Total:				
Portfolio:				
37.5% bonds; 62.5% stock	12.50%	$45,000	100.0%	100.0%
Composite Index:				
40% LBI; 60% S&P 500	15.54%			
Inflation (CPI)	3.25%			

If the account is taxable, this could reduce your return on an after-tax basis. Finally, and very importantly, the returns presented don't provide the slightest clue about how much risk you assumed to achieve them. This is crucial for you to know so you can evaluate the returns in a meaningful context.

13

RISK MEASUREMENT

Risk measurement can be summed up in two straightforward questions:
1. Are you comfortable with the risk you assume?
2. Are you getting paid for the risk you assume?

The questions are simple enough. The answers require you to examine a few numerical examples, so don't take off those armbands and that green eyeshade quite yet.

ARE YOU COMFORTABLE WITH THE RISK YOU ASSUME?

This question is personal for each of us. There is no right or wrong answer; there is a practical answer. If your investments cause you neither to lose sleep at night nor to reach for the Maalox when you read your monthly statements, you probably are investing within your comfort zone. If these or similar symptoms evince themselves, you probably are investing outside your comfort zone. Let's take a look at a few techniques for assessing your risk tolerance.

CURRENT PORTFOLIO

Actions speak louder than words, so your current holdings are a good place to start. Your current portfolio says a lot about your attitude toward risk assumption. If you hold high-yield debts or mostly stocks with allocations to either emerging-market or small-cap U.S. stocks, you may be on the bold, or risk-tolerant, end of the scale. On the other hand, if you hold mostly cash and investment-grade debts with a small allocation to large stocks, you may be on the timid, or risk-intolerant, end of the scale.

AVOCATIONS

This is one of my favorites because it is subject to such colorful interpretations. Investment advisers and brokers sometimes ask their clients how they spend their free time to gain a glimpse of their risk profiles. For instance, if you said you enjoyed fishing that might seem tame enough. However, there is an enormous difference in risk between spear fishing for great white sharks off Australia's Great Barrier Reef and fly fishing for brook trout in a New England stream. Similarly, if you said you enjoyed amusement parks, there is quite a difference in risk between riding the vomitron and the carousel. Finally, if you said that gaming in Las Vegas, also known as "Lost Wages," was your favorite pastime, there is little comparison in risk between bingo and table-stakes stud poker. At best, this kind of questioning is directional, but hardly conclusive.

RISK TESTING

Risk testing is the only tool I know of that purports to measure your ability to tolerate risk. It consists of a series of questions that are scored based on your responses. The sum of your scores is then placed on a continuum that ranges from very tolerant to intolerant. A typical risk test and its scoring continuum are shown in Figure 13-1.

Figure 13-1   RISK PROFILE

Instructions:

Answer the questions as accurately as possible. Some will require you to break down your investment accounts into asset classes and combine them.

1. What percent of your accounts is invested in individual stocks and stock mutual funds:
    a. Over 50%
    b. 20 to 50%
    c. Under 20%

2. What percent of your combined individual stocks and stock mutual funds is invested in U.S. large capitalization (S&P 500) companies:
    a. Under 60%
    b. 60 to 80%
    c. Over 80%

3. What percent of your fixed-income holdings of both individual securities and mutual funds is invested in issues with more than five years to maturity:
    a. Over 50%
    b. 20 to 50%
    c. Under 20%

4. How would you describe your attitude toward financial risk:
    a. Accept a high level for superior returns
    b. Accept a moderate level for above-average returns
    c. Avoid it altogether as you hate to lose

5. Most of the financial information upon which you base decisions comes from which sources:
    a. A blend of personal analysis and professional advice
    b. A blend of personal analysis and personal contacts
    c. Professional advice only

6. In selecting a stock for your portfolio, you most likely would choose:
 a. A new, small company with hot growth prospects
 b. A large, established company at a discount
 c. A large, established company at full price

7. You plan to leave at least 75% of your portfolio invested for:
 a. Over ten years
 b. Five to ten years
 c. Under five years

8. A stock you own reports disappointing earnings and comes under heavy selling pressure. The fundamentals of the business are otherwise unchanged. Your cost in this stock is $10,000 and it has declined to $7,500. Your broker or investment adviser calls and suggests the below options. Which do you choose:
 a. Hold six months with a 90% chance of selling at $10,000
 b. Hold four weeks with an 80% chance of selling at $9,000
 c. Sell immediately for $7,500 and take your lumps

9. Your boss offers your annual bonus of $20,000 in cash or company stock. You may not sell any bonus shares for five years and they pay no dividend. Based on management's expectations, the shares could triple in value over the next five years. Which option do you choose:
 a. Accept the entire bonus in shares
 b. Negotiate to take half in shares and half in cash
 c. Accept the entire bonus in cash

10. You own shares worth $40,000 in a U.S. large-cap mutual fund that has beaten the S&P 500 index by an average of 2% annually net of fees for the past ten years. This year the shares have declined 20% while the index is down 14%. Nothing else has changed. You would:
 a. Hold tight and possibly buy more
 b. Hold tight and monitor the fund closely
 c. Begin selling shares as you have lost faith in the manager

****

SCORING SUMMARY

a. = 10   Name:_____
b. = 5
c. = 0   Date:_____

           Score:_____

Apply the above values to your answers and add them together.

Score	Risk Profile
75 - 100	**Aggressive:** willing to tolerate high levels of risk
50 - 74	**Moderate:** willing to tolerate a blend of high and medium levels of risk
25 - 49	**Conservative:** willing to tolerate some medium level risk
0 - 24	**Intolerant:** unwilling to accept loss of principal, even temporarily

****

Your risk profile is useful information to both you and your investment-service providers. It is indicative of which asset classes and allocation percentages might work best for you within your comfort zone. Contrary to conventional investing wisdom, I have concluded empirically that risk profiles do not change significantly over an investor's lifetime. The investors I viewed as risk-tolerant in middle age have remained so in senior citizenship. Similarly, the investors I viewed as risk-intolerant in middle age have remained so in senior citizenship. I suspect the reason is that old habits and attitudes die hard, even when it concerns investing.

STRESS TESTING

This term is borrowed from the materials engineer's lexicon and refers to simulating and measuring responses to conditions of stress in a laboratory. It provides the data that aid in safely designing things like jet-engine vanes and critical auto parts before they are placed into service. Stress testing also can be applied to your investment portfolio. By looking at the historical variability and correlation of the asset classes you own, you can simulate a down-market case and estimate the impact in dollars. Let's take a look at the example in Table 13-1, which we'll give a scientific-sounding name like Case Gamma.

Table 13-1

Case Gamma
Stress Test
Your Portfolio
Long rate: +2%
S&P 500: -20%
(Rounded)

Asset Allocation	Before Stress		After Stress		Gain (Loss)
	%	$000s	%	$000s	$000s
Cash	10	25	12	25	
T-bonds: 6%, 20-yr.	30	75	31	66	(9)
Large-cap stocks	60	150	57	120	(30)
Total	100	250	100	211	(39)

Case Gamma is based on a 20% decline in the S&P 500 index accompanied by a 2% rise in the 20-year T-bond yield. There is no impact on cash. The price of debts is inverse to the yield, so the bonds' principal declined by some $9,000 in response to rising interest rates. The stocks declined at the same rate as the index, which produced a loss of $30,000. The overall impact on our hypothetical Case Gamma is a loss of $39,000, or almost 16% (-39,000/250,000 = -15.6). If this sort of loss level gets your stomach churning, you ought to consider shortening your bond maturities and lightening up on equities. If you can live with Case Gamma, you are within your comfort zone. In either case, some portfolio rebalancing might be needed to reach the revised or original target allocation percentages.

All these techniques can be helpful in answering our first question concerning risk tolerance. Like most psychological measures, there are no precise answers, but only points on a continuum.

ARE YOU GETTING PAID FOR THE RISK YOU ASSUME?

Our second question lends itself to more mathematically elegant measurement. Let's begin by looking at a few important concepts.

Volatility Of Returns

One common measure of overall risk is the variability, or **volatility**, of an investment's value over time. As noted before, modern portfolio theory holds that about a third of the risk of owning an individual security is related to the market in general. This is called systematic risk. The balance of the risk is specific to that individual security. This is called unsystematic risk. In the section on statistics, we looked at the price per ounce of gold over 11 years. We also calculated the volatility of the price of gold by comparing each June's price with the 11-year average price.

As you can see in Table 13-2, the mean, or average, price for these 11 annual observations is $383. The absolute range is -$42 to +$68. The range by itself suggests that the variability over the 11 years has been modest. Another common approach to evaluating gold's price variability is the standard deviation. In our example, the standard deviation is arrived at by adding together the squares of each year's price variability, dividing by the number of observations, and finding that result's square root: $(13,481/11)^{(1/2)} = 35.01$. I realize that this rivals cleaning the Augean stables for excitement, but please bear with me. It does get better.

Statisticians call this distribution of data bell-shaped, or normal. In a normal distribution, 68% of the observations lie one standard deviation below or above the mean. Let's test our 11 observations. By inspection you can see that seven, or 64% (7/11 = .636), of the observations are within $35.01 of the mean price of $383; four, or 36% (4/11 = .364), of the observations are not. This supports the conclusion that the 11 price observations form a normal distribution.

Table 13-2   London Gold
                           ($ Rounded)

June in Year	**P** Observed Price	**A** Average Price	**V = P - A** Variability of Price	**V^(2)** Squared Variability
87	450	383	67	4,489
88	451	383	68	4,624
89	367	383	-16	256
90	370	383	-13	169
91	367	383	-16	256
92	341	383	-42	1,764
93	372	383	-11	121
94	386	383	3	9
95	388	383	5	25
96	385	383	2	4
97	341	383	-42	1,764
Total	4,218			13,481

Average: 4,218/11 = 383.00
Standard Deviation: 35.01

The standard deviation, which encompasses both systematic and unsystematic risk, is a commonly used measure of an investment's price or rate-of-return volatility. The standard deviation of an investment's percentage rate of return can be compared directly and meaningfully with the standard deviation of the percentage rates of return of relevant market indices as well as alternative asset classes.

Beta Coefficient

The beta coefficient (Beta), which is named after the second letter in the Greek alphabet, is the measure of the extent to which a security's or portfolio's movements are related to the movements of its relevant benchmark. The Beta of the benchmark is always unity, or 1.00, and represents all the market, or systematic, risk. For instance, a large-cap stock whose returns rise and fall in exactly the same pattern as its benchmark, the S&P 500 index, has a Beta of 1.00. Similarly, a corporate bond whose returns rise and fall in exactly the same pattern as its benchmark, the Lehman Brothers aggregate index, has a Beta of 1.00. A less-volatile security has a Beta of less than 1.00; conversely, a more-volatile security has a Beta greater than 1.00. You would expect securities with Betas above 1.00 to fall more than the market as a whole in periods of declining prices. You also would expect securities with Betas above 1.00 to gain more than the market as a whole in periods of rising prices.

Risk Premium

The return that a portfolio earns in excess of the risk-free rate is called the risk premium. The risk-free rate is available from short-term U.S. Treasury debts, which are guaranteed against default by the federal government. The risk-free rate is the minimum return any investor would accept. For instance, if an investment earns 12% and the available risk-free rate is 4%, the excess return, or risk premium, is 8% (12 - 4 = 8). You might think of the risk premium as analogous to hazardous-duty pay. It explains why drivers of aviation-fuel trucks earn more than drivers of milk trucks. This is how you get paid for bearing increasing levels of risk.

Alpha Coefficient

The alpha coefficient (Alpha), which is named after the first letter in the Greek alphabet, is a measure that combines the concepts of the beta coefficient and excess return. It reveals the value added by portfolio decisions like security selection and timing, which are driven by the manager not the market in general. Let's look at an example in Table 13-3.

Table 13-3 Return & Risk
Your Portfolio
Year: '00

	Annual Return	Risk-free Rate	Excess Return	Standard Deviation	Beta
Portfolio	12.00%	4.50%	7.50%	10.00%	0.85
S&P 500	9.50%	4.50%	5.00%	12.00%	1

Let's say the risk-free U.S. Treasury bill rate is 4.5%. In order to isolate the value added to your portfolio by security selection and timing decisions, we must separate out market risk. This can be done by adjusting the excess return of the relevant index with the Beta of your portfolio. This result represents the excess return you would expect to receive based on the risk assumed in your portfolio. In Table 13-3, the excess return of the S&P 500 index is 5.00% and the Beta of your portfolio is 0.85. Your portfolio assumed a different level of risk than the index, so we must adjust the index return with the formula: EER = IER x PB, where "EER" is expected excess return, "IER" is index excess return and "PB" is your portfolio Beta. Applying the formula yields 4.25% (5.00 x .85 = 4.25).

Next, let's compare the excess return your portfolio actually produced with the expected excess return by applying the formula: Alpha = PER - EER, where "PER" is your portfolio's excess return and "EER" has been defined above. Applying the formula yields an Alpha of 3.25% (7.50 - 4.25 = 3.25). It is the value added by the manager of your portfolio and is in this case laudable. This is summarized in Table 13-4. This means that separate and apart from systematic risk, the manager contributed through security selection and timing an additional 3.25% in annual return to your portfolio. Now, there's a manager you want to have on your investment team! Naturally, a negative Alpha is a danger signal and indicates that you are not getting paid for the risk you are assuming. Incidentally, by definition the Alpha of a benchmark is always 0.00%. This is because the benchmark is unmanaged and has a Beta of unity, or 1.00. Hence, the formula for "EER" is a mathematical identity.

Table 13-4   Return & Risk
                              Your Portfolio
                                Year: '00

	Annual Return	Standard Deviation	R-squared	Beta	Alpha
Portfolio	12.00%	10.00%	0.93	0.85	3.25%
S&P 500	9.50%	12.00%	1	1	0.00%

R-SQUARED

I saved this until now because it will make more sense to you. In the section on statistics, we discussed the correlation coefficient in the context of investment behavior. As you recall, the correlation coefficient shows the degree to which two variable quantities are systematically connected. Perfect correlation has an R-squared of unity, or 1.00. The mathematical expression in spreadsheet protocol for the correlation coefficient is R^2. R-squared is very important in performance and risk measurement because all those neat comparisons to benchmarks presuppose that the benchmarks themselves are relevant, or highly correlated, to the measured security or portfolio. If R-squared is between, say, 0.80 and 1.00, the comparisons have high validity. If R-squared is less than 0.80, the comparisons have commensurately less validity. In Table 13-4 the R-squared is 0.93, which gives you a high level of confidence that the benchmark is relevant.

DURATION

Because interest-rate risk is so significant to debt investors, a mathematical tool called duration was developed to measure it in 1938 by Frederick Macaulay, an American economist. Duration represents the weighted-average term-to-maturity of a bond's cash flows. Duration is expressed in years and serves as a measurement of the sensitivity of a bond's price to changes in general interest rates. As we discovered in the chapter on debts, bond prices move in opposition to general interest rates.

Remember PITY? The calculation of duration for a noncallable bond that is ten years away from maturity and bears a 6%, semiannual coupon is shown in Table 13-5.

As you can see, the calculation of duration employs several of the concepts we discussed in earlier chapters including the weighted average and the present value formula. The duration of this bond is 7.6 years. Therefore, you would expect it to decline 7.6% in price for every 1% increase in market interest rates. Conversely, this same bond would be expected to rise 7.6% in price for every 1% decline in market interest rates. As this bond approaches maturity, its duration steadily declines, provided market interest rates remain at 6%.

A bond with identical features that is five years from maturity has a shorter duration. This is shown in Table 13-6. The five-year bond has a duration of 4.4 years, which makes it less sensitive to changes in market interest rates than a ten-year bond. If all other features are identical, the lower a bond's coupon rate, the greater its duration. As you might expect, the duration of a zero-coupon bond is equal to its maturity.

The duration of a debt portfolio is an indicator of the investor's conviction about the direction of future interest rates. As you can imagine, high-duration debt portfolios can provide you with a very turbulent ride.

SUMMARY OF RISK MEASUREMENT

The measures we have discussed here are the bare essentials for answering our second question concerning risk. More sophisticated approaches include focusing on only downside, or "bad," risk as opposed to upside, or "good," risk. For instance, *Business Week* has developed a system for rating mutual funds that penalizes a fund's rating for each month it failed to return at least as much as the risk-free T-bill rate. Recently, the SEC has begun accepting comments on how to better convey to the public the risk of investing in mutual funds. Morgan Stanley responded with a measure called M-squared, which is named after Nobel laureate Franco Modigliani and his granddaughter Leah, its talented developers. M-squared is arrived at by notionally diluting or leveraging with cash a fund's return until it matches the volatility of its benchmark. This is decidedly ingenious, but a little hard to grasp for most people. Additionally, a number of other sophisticated measurement tools have been developed and are available

Table 13-5

Duration
$1,000, 10-yr. Bond
Purchased: 01/01/98
Coupon: 6.00%
Semiannual Interest
(Rounded)

A No. of Periods	Year Ending	B Cash Flow	C P.V. Factor	B x C = D P.V.	A x D Weighted P.V.
1		30	0.97	29.1	29.1
2	12/31/98	30	0.94	28.2	56.4
3		30	0.92	27.6	82.8
4	12/31/99	30	0.89	26.7	106.8
5		30	0.86	25.8	129.0
6	12/31/00	30	0.84	25.2	151.2
7		30	0.81	24.3	170.1
8	12/31/01	30	0.79	23.7	189.6
9		30	0.77	23.1	207.9
10	12/31/02	30	0.74	22.2	222.0
11		30	0.72	21.6	237.6
12	12/31/03	30	0.70	21.0	252.0
13		30	0.68	20.4	265.2
14	12/31/04	30	0.66	19.8	277.2
15		30	0.64	19.2	288.0
16	12/31/05	30	0.62	18.6	297.6
17		30	0.61	18.3	311.1
18	12/31/06	30	0.59	17.7	318.6
19		30	0.57	17.1	324.9
20	12/31/07	1,030	0.55	566.5	11,330.0
Total				1,000.0	15,247.1

Duration: 15,247.1/(2 x 1,000.0) = 7.6

Table 13-6   Duration
                                     $1,000, 5-yr. Bond
                                    Purchased: 01/01/98
                                      Coupon: 6.00%
                                    Semiannual interest
                                        (Rounded)

A		B	C	B x C = D	A x D
No. of	Year	Cash			Weighted
Periods	Ending	Flow	P.V. Factor	P.V.	P.V.
1		30	0.97	29.1	29.1
2	12/31/98	30	0.94	28.2	56.4
3		30	0.92	27.6	82.8
4	12/31/99	30	0.89	26.7	106.8
5		30	0.86	25.8	129.0
6	12/31/00	30	0.84	25.2	151.2
7		30	0.81	24.3	170.1
8	12/31/01	30	0.79	23.7	189.6
9		30	0.77	23.1	207.9
10	12/31/02	1,030	0.74	762.2	7,622.0
Total				1,000.0	8,744.9

Duration: 8,744.9/(2 x 1,000.0) = 4.4

by contacting AIMR in Charlottesville, Virginia. If your appetite for these subjects is still not satisfied, I strongly recommend a recently published book called *Measuring Investment Performance* (McGraw-Hill, 1997) by David Spaulding. It does an excellent job of covering the current trends in the industry. As we complete this section on risk measurement, bear in mind that all these measurement tools except duration are backward-looking. Very little in investing remains constant over time, so the measurement tools discussed here may have limited predictive value. Finally, avoiding high levels of risk may be a luxury you can ill afford. If your assets must reach a certain value to pay for college or ensure a comfortable retirement income, you might be forced to assume more risk than you like to grow your wealth adequately. Unhappily, sometimes the more turbulent ride is your only acceptable option.

14

SYNTHESIS

Whew! The finish line is finally in sight. Now comes the time to see how investing works in real life. Let's roll up our sleeves and apply our knowledge to constructing three hypothetical portfolios that address the most common investment goals that people have. They are:

1. A home down payment
2. A child's college education
3. A comfortable retirement income

Before we address these three cases, let's step back and define a time-horizon framework for investing. Investing can be divided into two distinct phases. The first is accumulation, in which you begin with little or no assets and grow your wealth. The second is liquidation, in which you spend or transfer your assets either all at once or over time. In some cases, these phases are separated in time; in other cases, these phases overlap in time. Additionally, the longer the time horizon, the more difficult it is to grasp the impact of inflation on purchasing power and the effect of compounding on investment returns. With that in mind, let's tackle our three cases.

A HOME DOWN PAYMENT

Investing for a home down payment consists of an accumulation phase followed by a single liquidation to fund the payment. Let's say that Jennifer and Robert, a couple in their middle twenties, decide to begin saving for a house that currently costs $150,000. Because they wish to obtain the best available mortgage terms and avoid **private mortgage insurance (PMI)**, they are prepared to save 20% of the purchase price as a down payment. They sit down with a friendly lender, Mortgages R Us, and discover that based on current residential real-estate inflation the $150,000 house they fancy will rise in cost about 4.5% per year. Thus, using the now familiar rule of 72, they estimate its cost will double in about 16 (72/4.5 = 16) years or rise half that amount, or 50%, in about 8 or 9 (36/4.5 = 8) years. Robert and Jennifer resolve to begin saving next month with a target home purchase date of nine years. At that time, they project the house will cost about $225,000 (150,000 x 1.5 = 225,000), so they will need $45,000 (.2 x 225,000 = 45,000) to cover the down payment. After much spirited discussion, which tests the very fabric of their commitment to each other, they decide to live within a budget, which Jennifer agrees to develop.

After interviewing several investment professionals, they hire Isabella Partial, CPA/PFS, to produce an investment plan on a fee-only basis. First, Isabella suggests that they take a written risk test that will serve as an indicator of their joint willingness to bear risk. They score an 85%, which is very risk-tolerant. Additionally, Isabella determines that Jennifer and Robert will be in the 28% **marginal** income-tax bracket for at least the next five years.

Next, Isabella helps her new clients determine how much they must save per month to reach their goal of at least $45,000 in nine years. She cautions them that despite their high tolerance for risk, nine years is a marginally short investment time horizon based on historical equity-market indices. She further admonishes them that it is possible for equities to lose value for temporary periods of several years. They decide to let Isabella compute the monthly savings requirement under different rate-of-return assumptions to better determine how to proceed. The next morning, Isabella boots up her investment calculation software and in a billable jiffy computes the monthly savings requirements for the range of asset classes reflected in Table 14-1.

Table 14-1   Jennifer & Robert
                                   Investment Plan
                              $45,000 net in 9 years
                                Data: 1926-1997
                                    (Rounded)

Asset Class	Average Annual Return	% of 5-year Holding Periods Showing Loss	Standard Deviation	Required Monthly Savings
Large-cap stocks	11%	10%	20%	$246
Small-cap stocks	13%	13%	34%	$221
Long Corp. Bonds	6%	4%	9%	$315
Long T-bonds	5%	9%	9%	$331
Intermed. T-bonds	5%	0%	6%	$331
Risk-free T-bills	4%	0%	3%	$347
Inflation	3%	10%	5%	n/a

Upon reviewing these data, Jennifer and Robert marvel at how easy it will be to reach $45,000 in nine years by investing in small-cap stocks. Setting aside a mere $221 per month gets the job done and doesn't cramp their spending style nearly as much as they had feared. Isabella hastens to remind them that the total return of small-cap stocks not only exhibited an average annual standard deviation of 34% since 1926, but also lost money in 13% of the 68 five-year periods ending on or before December 31, 1997. Robert cavalierly asserts that you can't take risk-adjusted returns to the bank, whereupon Jennifer wades in and stonily asks Isabella to continue her presentation with an emphasis on risk.

Isabella walks them through the table and concludes by recommending a balanced portfolio of 50% large-cap value stocks yielding 3.00% and 50% low-duration, intermediate T-bonds yielding 5.00%. Because they are starting from scratch, Isabella agrees to help them select no-load mutual funds that feature low initial investment requirements, a reinvestment option, and an **automatic monthly contribution** plan. This asset mix represents a low-risk approach, but still has a historical average annual total return of 8% [(11 + 5)/2 = 8]. Isabella patiently explains that this asset mix has both a lower standard deviation and a lower chance of producing a loss in any five-year holding period. She also points out the low cross-correlation between large-cap stocks and intermediate bonds. Since Jennifer and Robert have a fixed goal of $45,000, the reduced risk of temporary loss is attractive to them.

Isabella reruns the investment calculation software and determines that contributing $286 per month before taxes and fees will get the job done. Upon hearing this, Jennifer asks what Isabella means by "before taxes and fees." Isabella explains that since this account will be fully taxable, she will have to net down the average annual total return to account for estimated annual fees and expenses of 1% as well as income taxes. She further explains that they could use an **individual retirement account (IRA)** as the investment vehicle, but she would prefer they plan not to touch any IRA funds and get a jump on building up their retirement savings. Jennifer and Robert agree to proceed with a taxable account and Isabella reruns the numbers by netting down the average annual total return from 8% as shown in Table 14-2. Happily, the results are not too bad! After netting out fees of 1% and applying assumed tax rates for stock dividends, long-term capital gains and bond interest of 28%, 20% and 28%, respectively, the projected weighted-average annual total return net of fees and taxes is 5.08% [(.5 x 7.56) + (.5 x 2.60) = 5.08]. This produces a monthly savings requirement of $330, which is still manageable for Jennifer and Robert.

Isabella concludes her assignment by identifying a large-cap value index fund and a diversified intermediate T-bond fund with low initial investment requirements, reinvestment options, and an automatic contribution plan. She suggests that Jennifer and Robert reduce their investment plan to writing, rebalance the portfolio annually by adjusting the contribution pattern if the asset mix changes more than 5%, and schedule an annual review with her to gauge progress toward their goal. She also presents them with an invoice for $250, which they plan to pay as soon as they get paid next month.

Table 14-2   Jennifer & Robert
Investment Plan
$45,000 net in 9 year
(Rounded)

Annual Taxes:

Asset Allocation	Avg. Annual Return	Stocks: 3%@.28 + 8%@.20 = 2.44% Bonds: 5%@.28 = 1.4%	Net Annual Fees	Total Return	Required Monthly Savings
Stocks: 50%	11%	(2.44%)	(1%)	7.56%	
Bonds: 50%	5%	(1.40%)	(1%)	2.60%	
Portfolio				5.08%	$330

A CHILD'S COLLEGE EDUCATION

Investing for a child's college education consists of an accumulation phase followed by a multi-year liquidation to fund the payments. Let's say Marsha and Gordon, a couple in their middle thirties, have a retirement plan in place and decide to start a college account for Kara, their three-year-old daughter. They do a little research and discover that private undergraduate college tuition, room and board runs about $25,000 per year and is projected to rise at about 4% per year. Marsha sits down at the family computer and uses a spreadsheet and her knowledge of compounding to jigger up the projected cost shown in Table 14-3.

Marsha rechecks the figures and calmly informs Gordon that their darling daughter's undergraduate education will cost nearly $200,000. After some vague remark about the possibility of an athletic scholarship, Gordon agrees to make an appointment the very next day with Isabella Partial, CPA/PFS. Gordon correctly senses that their joint savings account of $10,000, with which he eventually hoped to purchase the mother of all bass boats and a custom trailer to haul it, is in serious jeopardy.

Table 14-3   Kara's College Account
Projected Cost
Age 3: 09/01/98
(Rounded)

School Year	Years Remaining	Inflation Factor@4%	Current Cost	Future Cost
'14	16	1.87	$ 25,000	$ 46,750
'15	17	1.95	25,000	48,750
'16	18	2.03	25,000	50,750
'17	19	2.11	25,000	52,750
Total			$100,000	$199,000

After meeting with Isabella Partial and explaining their investment goal, she asks them to take a risk test. They jointly score a 40%, which places them on the conservative end of the risk-tolerance continuum. Additionally, Isabella determines that they expect to remain in the 31% marginal income-tax bracket, have accumulated savings of $10,000 in bank CDs that mature in 30 days, and are already funding a sensible retirement program. Isabella looks over Marsha's calculations and suggests that the $10,000 bank CDs be used to start the account. A crestfallen Gordon futilely attempts to conceal his disappointment as the specter of postponing the coveted bass boat looms. Isabella then proposes that the investment target should be an additional $190,000 in 16 years to ensure that the entire $200,000 is available by Kara's freshman year. She presents and carefully gauges their reaction to Table 14-4.

Both Marsha and Gordon register surprise at how much they must save on top of their IRAs and employer retirement accounts. Isabella explains that the 16-year time horizon permits them to take the risk of 100% equities, but recognizes that their conservative joint risk profile is at odds with this approach. She explains that the odds of a 15-year period producing a loss in equities is historically very low. She also suggests that they title the assets in Kara's name in an **Uniform Transfer to Minors**

157

Act (UTMA) account due to the fact that Kara no longer will be subject to their 31% income-tax bracket after the age of 14. This will give them from four to seven years during which long-term capital gains can be realized at a rate as low as 10%. Additionally, the savings-account balance and monthly contributions to Kara's UTMA account are well below the annual joint gift-tax exclusion of $20,000. She further explains that the Education IRA enacted in 1997 has a contribution limit of $500 per year, which is far short of their projected requirement.

Table 14-4

Kara's College Account
Beg. Bal.: $10,000
$200,000 in 16 Years
Data: 1926-1997
(Rounded)

Asset Class	Average Annual Return	% of 15-year Holding Periods Showing Loss	Standard Deviation	Required Monthly Savings
Large-cap stocks	11%	0%	20%	$274
Small-cap stocks	13%	5%	34%	$189
Long Corp. Bonds	6%	0%	9%	$542
Long T-bonds	5%	0%	9%	$606
Intermed. T-bonds	5%	0%	6%	$606
Risk-free T-bills	4%	0%	3%	$675
Inflation	3%	5%	5%	n/a

Isabella cautions them that as custodians they will not be permitted to use the money for other purposes such as a nifty, new bass boat. She further admonishes them that when Kara reaches majority, she will be legally entitled to abandon her education and travel the Tibet Freedom Concert circuit until she runs out of money. After answering their questions about the risks and duties of a custodian, Isabella presents the proposed investment plan shown in Table 14-5.

Table 14-5   Kara's UTMA Account
Beg. Bal.: $10,000
$200,000 in 16 Years
(Rounded)

Asset Allocation	Average Annual Return	Annual Taxes: L-cap: 2%@.15+9%@.1 S-cap: 13%@.1 Munis: 0%	Annual Fees	Net Total Return	Required Monthly Savings
Large-cap: 50%	11%	(1.20%)	(1%)	8.80%	
Small-cap: 20%	13%	(1.30%)	(1%)	10.70%	
Munis: 30%	4%	n/a	(1%)	3.00%	
Portfolio				7.44%	$456

Isabella explains that the proposed portfolio consists of 70% equity mutual funds and 30% tax-exempt Munis and has a projected weighted-average annual total return net of fees and taxes of 7.44% [(.5 x 8.80) + (.2 x 10.70) + (.3 x 3.00) = 7.44]. It requires $456 per month for the next 16 years to fund. Gordon utters a sigh as he resigns himself to the inevitable and uxoriously capitulates. Marsha squeezes his hand consolingly as the color drains from his face. Isabella further clarifies that the large-cap and small-cap equity funds, which provide the bulk of the return, should be tax-efficient, so that a large portion of their long-term capital gains can be realized systematically after Kara reaches 14 and is subject to her own rate of as low as 10%. She explains that the investment-grade Munis reduce overall volatility due to their low cross-correlation to both equity asset classes. They also provide a steady income stream, which avoids their 31% tax bracket to which Kara is subject until age 14.

Finally, Isabella suggests that they monitor the unrealized gains in the equity funds and begin to consider **dollar-cost averaging** out of the market when Kara reaches 16. This approach will ensure that the cash is available when needed and that no single year's realized capital gains will drive up Kara's income-tax rate unnecessarily. The funds released in this orderly liquidation can be invested in zero-coupon bonds or **target-maturity debt** mutual funds pending payment of annual college costs.

After some discussion, Marsha and Gordon approve the plan. Isabella concludes her assignment by developing a shortlist of no-load equity mutual funds that have done an excellent job of minimizing income taxes as well as an intermediate-term, investment-grade municipal-bond fund. All the funds offer a reinvestment option and an automatic contribution plan. She suggests that Marsha and Gordon reduce the investment plan to writing, rebalance the portfolio annually by adjusting the pattern of contributions if the asset mix changes more than 5%, and schedule an annual review with her to gauge progress toward their goal. She also presents them with an invoice for $500, which they plan to pay as soon as they get home.

A COMFORTABLE RETIREMENT INCOME

Investing for a comfortable retirement income typically consists of a long accumulation phase followed by an overlapping, multi-decade liquidation phase to fund the income. Let's say Kelly and Chris, a genial and frugal couple in their middle forties with two teenagers, make a New Year's resolution to figure out how well prepared they are for retirement. After several months of studious procrastination, Chris, at Kelly's urging, decides to sit down and run the numbers. After several frustrating evenings of poring over financial spreadsheets and a computerized retirement planner from a mutual-fund distributor, Chris calls Isabella Partial, CPA/PFS, and makes an appointment.

Isabella agrees to meet them both and asks them to bring along their savings and retirement-account statements as well as their past two years' tax returns. After a lengthy interview, Isabella ascertains that Kelly and Chris both work for a successful cheese producer and have a joint income before taxes of $75,000, which places them in the 28% marginal income-tax bracket. She also learns that they have ten years remaining on their home mortgage, have saved adequately for both children's college educations in UTMA accounts, and have in their own names the net worth shown in Figure 14-1.

Figure 14-1
Kelly & Chris
Net Worth Statement
At: 06/01/98

Assets		**Liabilities**		
Current:		Current:		
Cash	$ 2,000	Bills on hand	$	600
Long-term:		Taxes owed		400
Brokerage a/c	25,000	Credit cards		1,000
Autos	12,000	Long-term:		
Pers. property	15,000	Auto loans		3,000
Residence	180,000	Mortgage		32,000
IRAs	75,000			
401(k)s	80,000	Total Liabilities		37,000
		Net worth		352,000
Total	$389,000	Total		$389,000

After additional discussion, Isabella concludes that the brokerage account, IRAs and 401(k)s, which total $180,000, should be viewed as a single portfolio for retirement purposes. She also learns that Kelly and Chris are disinclined to leave their two children a large sum of money apart from their personal residence, which will be fully paid for by then. Isabella informs her clients that since all their parents are living and in good health, they should expect to live to age 90 for planning purposes despite the shorter projected life spans contained in the current mortality tables. She further determines that they are prepared to contribute up to 10% of their gross income annually toward their retirement, plan to work 20 more years until they both reach 66, and have adequate life, health and disability insurance in place.

Isabella hands them a risk test on which they jointly score a 60%, which places them on the moderately tolerant end of the risk-tolerance continuum. She also explains that most retirees find that they can live very comfortably on 70–80% of their pre-retirement gross income unless they move to a higher-cost area. Kelly and Chris assure her that they plan to live out their years in Mukwonago, Wisconsin, so that should not be a problem. Additionally, Isabella points out that during retirement all qualified withdrawals from the regular IRAs and 401(k)s will be treated as fungible from a tax perspective and taxed at ordinary rates, not the lower capital-gains rates. Finally, she observes that their joint Social Security income almost certainly will be taxable due to the magnitude of their income from retirement vehicles. Accordingly, Isabella concludes that expressing the plan in pre-tax dollars makes the most sense and permits comparison to their current joint salaries.

The following week, Kelly and Chris arrive punctually at Isabella's office, whereupon she presents to them the worksheet shown in Figure 14-2 and the accompanying explanatory comments.

1. *Target annual gross retirement income of $131,000.* This was arrived at by adjusting your current gross income for 4% annual inflation over the next 20 years and applying a conservative 80% factor: (75,000 x 2.19 x .8 = 131,000). It is expressed in dollars of 2018.

2. *Expected annual gross Social Security benefit of $55,000.* This was arrived at by adjusting your current personalized Social Security benefit estimates for 4% annual inflation over the next 20 years: (25,000 x 2.19 = 55,000). It also is expressed in dollars of 2018. Social Security is indexed for inflation during retirement, so there is no need to further adjust this figure beyond dollars of 2018.

3. *Retirement income gap of $76,000.* This is the difference between the target annual gross retirement income of $131,000 and the expected gross annual Social Security benefit of $55,000: (131,000 - 55,000 = 76,000).

4. *Required portfolio value of $1,267,000.* This value was derived by dividing a depletion factor of 6%, or .06, into the retirement income gap of $76,000: (76,000/.06 = 1,267,000). The depletion factor was generated by a mathematical model into which the inflation rate, investment return net of fees, and years during retirement are fed. In this case, the values used were 4%, 8% and 25 years, respectively. The depletion factor is based on your receiving before taxes 6% of the required portfolio value of $1,267,000, or $76,000, per year beginning in 2018 and an additional

Figure 14-2

Kelly & Chris
Retirement Plan
At: 06/01/98
($ Rounded)

Current income	75,000		Expected	
x Growth factor			return	9.00%
@4% = 2.19	164,000		Less:	
x .80		131,000	Fees	(1.00%)
Less:			Inflation	(4.00%)
Social Security	(25,000)		Real return	4.00%
x Growth factor				
(25,000 x 2.19)		(55,000)		
Retirement				
income gap		76,000	Depletion	25 Yrs.
Required			Indicated %	
portfolio value			withdrawal	
(76,000/.06)		1,267,000	to depletion	6.00%
Less:				
Current savings				
20 years @ 8%				
(180,000 x 4.66)		(839,000)		
Retirement				
investment gap		428,000		
Monthly requirement		752		
Less:				
Employer matching				
(6% x 75,000 x 50%)/12		(188)		
Net requirement		564		

4% each year thereafter to maintain constant purchasing power. The factor further assumes that the entire portfolio value of $1,267,000 is depleted to zero in 25 years. In other words, at age 90 you depart this life broke!

Alternatively, it is possible to estimate the required portfolio value with a simple financial calculator by entering the monthly retirement income gap as a negative number, the number of months during retirement, and the portfolio rate of return net of fees and inflation. These values are - $6,333 (76,000/12 = 6,333), 300 months (25 x 12 = 300), and 4% [(9 - (1 + 4) = 4], respectively. The resulting estimated required portfolio value is $1,209,000. This result is within 5% [(1,267,000 - 1,209,000)/ 1,267,000 = 4.6] of the more precise method above, which is arguably close enough for most purposes.

5. *Current savings reduction of $839,000.* This amount was derived by applying an 8% annual growth rate net of fees only to the current total savings of $180,000: (180,000 x 4.66 = 839,000). It is expressed in dollars of 2018 and includes the brokerage account, IRAs and 401(k)s.

6. *Retirement investment gap of $428,000.* This is the difference between the required portfolio value of $1,267,000 and the current savings reduction of $839,000: (1,267,000 - 839,000 = 428,000). It is expressed in dollars of 2018.

7. *Monthly requirement of $752.* This is the monthly contribution required for the next 20 years to fund the retirement investment gap of $428,000 based on an 8% annual return net of fees. It was derived by using the compound interest formula and is expressed in dollars of 1998.

8. *Monthly employer matching of $188.* This amount is based on the employer 401(k) plan document, which provides for 50% matching of employee contributions up to 6% of gross salary subject to the current IRS limitation. Since Kelly and Chris are below the limitation, employer matching amounts to $188: [(.06 x 75,000 x .50)/12 = 188]. It is expressed in dollars of 1998.

9. *Monthly net requirement of $564.* Finally, this is the difference between the monthly contribution requirement of $752 and the monthly employer matching of $188: (752 - 188 = 564). It also is expressed in dollars of 1998.

After Kelly and Chris have reviewed these materials, Isabella explains that she happily was able to stay within their stated limit of 10% of gross salary, or $625 [(75,000/12) x .1 = 625]. This was due mainly to her belief that political pressure and sound federal fiscal policy will not permit the Social Security System to abandon its contributors. She also points out that in future years, with normal salary growth, the $564 will decline further as a percentage of their gross income. She further explains that this approach is more conservative because the higher contributions start immediately and compound longer. Isabella then presents Table 14-6 to them.

Table 14-6
Kelly & Chris
Gap: $428,000
Data: 1926-1997
(Rounded)

Asset Class	Average Annual Return	% of 20-year Holding Periods Showing Loss	Standard Deviation	Required Monthly Savings
Large-cap stocks	11%	0%	20%	$ 529
Small-cap stocks	13%	0%	34%	$ 416
Long Corp. Bonds	6%	0%	9%	$ 944
Long T-bonds	5%	0%	9%	$1,055
Intermed. T-bonds	5%	0%	6%	$1,055
Risk-free T-bills	4%	0%	3%	$1,176
Inflation	3%	0%	5%	n/a

She thoughtfully explains that their accumulation time horizon is really closer to 45 years than 20 years because they will remain fully invested throughout the liquidation phase of their retirement. She also points out that over time horizons longer than 20 years, the major asset classes never have shown a loss. She states that even if there is a temporary loss as they approach age 90, they can draw on the equity in their home to supplement their income. The children almost certainly will not choose to remain in Mukwonago, so a small mortgage should pose no problem when the home is sold ultimately. Lastly, she enumerates the reasons for investing in T-bonds and foreign securities and their importance due to low cross-correlation in her suggested asset-allocation model.

Chris advises Isabella that the Mukwonago CheeseWorks, their employer, has a bright new chief financial officer named Francine Fromage, who recently expanded the **401(k) menu** to ten choices of investments. As Chris understands it, they include all the major asset classes. Based on Kelly's and Chris' joint risk tolerance and investment objectives, Isabella presents the investment plan shown in Table 14-7. She explains that the projected weighted-average annual total return net of fees is 8.4% [(.3 x 10) + (.2 x 10) + (.1 x 12) + (.2 x 7) + (.2 x 4) = 8.4]. However, to be on the safe side, she has reduced it by 40 basis points to present a conservative case at 8%. She also explains that investment planning with long time horizons is based necessarily on crude estimates, so Kelly and Chris should not place unwarranted faith in her projections. The key is monitoring continuously the progress toward their goal including the status of the Social Security System.

After weighing the pros and cons of foreign stocks and long T-bonds, Isabella gets the nod from Kelly and Chris to allocate the current $180,000 as shown in Table 14-7. She suggests holding the T-bonds in the 401(k)s to avoid current income taxes. She also suggests holding small-cap and foreign stocks in the tax-deferred IRAs or 401(k)s because turnover is likely to be higher, resulting in more short-term gains.

Kelly and Chris agree to adjust their monthly 401(k) contributions to ensure that the totals including employer matching conform to the target asset allocation. They also agree to cease funding the brokerage account and IRAs since they are less advantageous than the 401(k) plans. Lastly, Isabella suggests that she provide Kelly and Chris a written **Investment Policy Statement (IPS)** that outlines their investment objectives, asset-allocation scheme and appropriate benchmarks for performance measurement. As they depart, Isabella suggests they meet annually around tax time to review the IPS, rebalance the portfolio by adjusting the pattern of contributions if the asset classes change more than 5%, and gauge progress toward their goal. She also presents them with an invoice for $1,000, which they pay on the spot.

Table 14-7   Kelly & Chris
                         Gap: $428,000
                         (Rounded)

Asset Allocation	Average Annual Return	Annual Fees	Average Net Total Return	Conservative Net Total Return
Large-cap: 30%	11%	(1%)	10%	
Mid-cap: 20%	11%	(1%)	10%	
Small-cap: 10%	13%	(1%)	12%	
Foreign: 20%	8%	(1%)	7%	
Long T-bond: 20%	5%	(1%)	4%	
Portfolio			8.4%	8%
Monthly requirement			$718	$752

OBSERVATIONS ON SYNTHESIS

Hopefully, the suggested solutions to these three hypothetical cases contain by now familiar approaches and concepts. There is, of course, a range of solutions that will work effectively in each case rather than a single, correct one. Also, note that each of the couples sought competent, professional investment advice before proceeding with a plan. More often than not, two heads are better than one when it comes to successful investing. Your discipline in saving, knowledge of your own risk tolerance, and persistence in prosecuting the investment plan are as important as the professionals whom you select to help you.

15

PARTING REMARKS

Well, we have come a long way together. You have mastered a lot of concepts and endured a lot of numbers in your efforts to cut the Gordian knot of understanding investing. I am very proud of how indefatigable a learner you have proven to be. To quote Benjamin Franklin, "Education is an implement, not an ornament." Now, it is time for you to apply your understanding of investing as you confront in your own life the challenge of developing a successful investment program.

You may elect to delegate your investment program entirely to professionals. If you do, choose them as painstakingly as you would your close friends and monitor carefully their results. On the other hand, you may elect to participate actively in your investment program with more limited professional assistance. If you do, continue your learning with the same assiduity that you exhibited in completing this book. In either case, may the tools that you have acquired from this book serve you well.

Should you have a question or comment about the contents of this book, I can be reached anytime on the dedicated Web site: www.gordianknot.org. My replies will be prompt, brief, and free of charge to any reader of *Cutting the Gordian Knot: Understanding Investing*.

GLOSSARY

Absolute: The numerical value of a quantity without regard to its sign.

Accounts payable: Liabilities consisting of unpaid bills owed by a business to its suppliers.

Accounts receivable: Assets consisting of unpaid billings owed to a business by its customers.

Accreted, interest: Interest that increases gradually over time.

Accrued payroll: Wages and salaries of employees that have been earned, but not paid.

Acquisition: Purchase of a business' assets or stock by another business.

Alternative minimum tax (AMT): Federal income tax imposed on taxpayers whose regular tax is lower because of certain deductions. These deductions are called tax preference items.

American depositary receipts (ADRs): Receipts for shares of a foreign company that trade on U.S. exchanges.

American depositary shares (ADSs): Shares of a foreign company that trade on U.S. exchanges.

Amortization, bonds: The systematic disappearance over time of a bond discount or premium.

Amplitude: The breadth or range of a set of values.

Annuitant: A person who receives—or is qualified to receive—an annuity.

Annuitization: The liquidation through periodic payments of an annuity contract over from at least five years to a lifetime.

Anticipations: The sale of assets prior to their legitimate availability, especially in the cases of trust funds and testamentary bequests.

Anti-dilution(ive): An act of a corporation that reduces the number of shares outstanding, e.g., a share buyback, thus increasing EPS.

Arithmetic mean: The average arrived at by summing a set of values and dividing by the number of values in the set.

Arrearage: An overdue payment, especially preferred stock dividends, that prevents common stockholders from receiving dividends.

Asset allocation: An investing approach that advocates the ownership of various asset classes that have low correlation with each other in order to maximize risk-adjusted returns.

Assets: Things an investor or business owns as a component of wealth.

Assets under management (AUM): The total market value of assets that an investment adviser supervises. AUM often serves as the base for computing fees.

Automatic monthly contribution: A monthly payment made directly from an investor's bank account to a mutual fund.

Basis point: A unit of measurement consisting of one hundredth of a percent.

Bearish: Pessimistic about the future direction of security prices. The opposite of bullish.

Beneficiary: A person or legal entity that receives—or is qualified to receive—the proceeds of a life-insurance policy.

Bimodal: A set of values that has two distinct statistical modes.

Bonds: A form of long-term indebtedness issued by government agencies, municipalities and corporations.

Book value: The difference between total assets and total liabilities. Also, net worth or shareholders' equity.

Bottom-up: An approach to security analysis that primarily looks at microeconomic data, companies and their prospects.

Bullish: Optimistic about the future direction of security prices. The opposite of bearish.

Call: The act of redeeming for cash securities that are callable.

Call feature: A security provision that permits conversion to cash based on events or the passage of time.

Call option: A contract that entitles the owner to purchase, or call away, securities at a set price for a specified period of time.

Callable, bonds: Bonds that contain a call feature.

Callable, preferred stock: Preferred stock that contains a call feature.

Capital: Wealth in the form of money or property.

Capital gains, tax: The preferential tax imposed on the profit that an investor derives by selling an asset at a price greater than its cost.

Capital structure: The relationship between stockholders' equity and debt in a corporation.

Category killer: A business that dominates a market segment on a national or international basis.

Charter: The legal document that creates and defines the powers of a corporation.

Chartist: An analyst of securities who places primary weight on charts and graphic records to predict price trends.

Closed-end: An investment company with fixed capitalization that does not permit entrance of new investors.

Common stock: The shares of ownership in a corporation.

Compound interest: Interest that is calculated on principal plus interest to date.

Consumer price index (CPI): The measure of inflation published monthly by the Department of Labor Statistics.

Contestability period: The initial two-year period during which a life insurer may refuse to pay a death benefit if the insured made a fraudulent or misleading statement on the policy application.

Contract owner: The person to whom an insurance or annuity contract belongs.

Convertible: The feature of securities, especially bonds and preferred stock, that permits exchange for common shares under specified circumstances.

Correlation coefficient: The statistical measure of the interdependence of two variables ranging from -1 to +1.

Cost-flow assumption: The method used to account for the use of items from inventory and charged to cost of goods sold. Also, the method used to account for the sale of securities purchased at different prices.

Cost of goods sold: The costs associated with goods or services that have been billed as revenue.

Coupon: The annual interest paid by the issuer of a debt security.

Covered options: Option contracts wherein the writer owns the underlying securities.

Covering: The act of unwinding a short sale by replacing the borrowed stock.

Credit risk: The probability a debt issuer will fail to pay interest or principal on time. See default risk.

Croesus: An ancient Lydian king, who was famed for his wealth.

Cross-correlation: The degree to which two or more asset classes move in the same pattern over time.

Current assets: Assets that are or will become cash within one year.

Current liabilities: Debts that must be settled in cash within one year.

Custodian: A person or business that safekeeps property, especially securities and cash.

Declare: The legal act of a corporation's board of directors in approving a dividend.

Deep discount: A price for a security that is well below its known or expected future value.

Default: The failure of a debt issuer to pay interest or principal on time.

Default risk: The probability a debt issuer will fail to pay interest or principal on time. See credit risk.

Deleveraging: The reduction of debt or increasing of equity in the capital structure of a person or business.

Depreciation: The accounting recognition of the wasting over time of tangible assets, especially plant and equipment.

Depression: A period of prolonged decline in economic activity that leads to unemployment and falling asset values.

Derivatives: Synthetic securities that derive their value from an underlying measure, e.g., foreign-currency rates, interest rates, stock or commodity prices, etc.

Dilute: To cause the number of a corporation's outstanding common shares to increase, thus decreasing EPS.

Dilution: The result of causing the number of a corporation's outstanding common shares to increase, thus decreasing EPS.

Discount, bonds: The amount for which a bond trades below its face amount.

Discount brokers: Securities brokers who charge very low fees or commissions and provide low levels of service.

Discount, equities: The state of a stock that trades at a lesser P/E ratio than its benchmark or relevant index.

Discount formula: $PV = FV[(1/(1 + i)^n)]$, where "PV" is present value, "FV" is future value, "i" is the assumed interest rate and "n" is the number of years. See present value.

Dividends: Cash or stock paid to shareholders proportionately as part of the reward for ownership.

Dollar-cost averaging: An investing technique that is based on contributing to or withdrawing from securities or mutual funds equal dollar amounts at regular intervals.

Double taxation: The penalty on distributed corporate earnings that are taxed first at the corporate level and again at the shareholder level.

Double tax-exempt: The tax status of interest on municipal debt that is exempt from federal and state income taxes.

Dow Jones industrial average (DJIA): An unweighted index based on 30 large-cap U.S. stocks that serves as a barometer of the market as a whole.

Earnings: The annual profit of a business that results from subtracting all expenses from revenues.

Earnings multiple: The market value per share of a stock divided by it's annual earnings per share. See P/E ratio.

Earnings per share (EPS): The quotient of a corporation's annual profits divided by its total common shares outstanding.

Econometrics: The application of quantitative and statistical techniques to the study of economics, especially with computer models.

Economies of scale: The lowering of cost per unit by increasing volume while some costs remain unchanged, e.g., rent and management salaries.

Elevator shafted: Fell like a stone, especially security prices.

Emerging: The status of nations that have low degrees of economic development.

Equity: The residual value of property beyond any debt or mortgage thereon; also, a synonym for common stock.

Errors and omissions (E&O) insurance: Insurance carried by service providers that protects client accounts from employee mistakes.

Exchange: A forum for the buying and selling of assets, especially securities.

Exchange fees: Fees imposed by a mutual-fund company on investors who switch monies among that company's fund offerings.

Exclusion ratio: The ratio of the nontaxable to the taxable components of the distributions from an annuity.

Expenses: Expired costs that reduce profit in the income statement.

Exponential: A curve that rises at an increasing rate.

Face amount: The amount reflected on the face of a security, especially bonds, without regard to a discount or premium.

Fiduciaries: Persons or corporations who stand in a special relationship of trust and legal obligation to others.

Financial accounting: The area of accounting concerned with the production of financial statements.

Fixed charges: Business expenses that must be paid periodically regardless of the level of business activity, e.g., interest on debt.

Form ADV: The SEC document that must be completed annually by registered investment advisers.

401(k) menu: The range of investment choices offered in a 401(k) plan.

Fully taxable: The status of enjoying no tax exemption on income or capital gains.

Fund-of-funds: A fund that invests in other funds' shares for diversification or asset-allocation purposes.

Fund return: The return of a mutual fund associated with an investment that is not subject to the contributions and withdrawals of the investor, but remains invested for the entire period.

Fundamental, analysis: Security analysis based on factors intrinsic to a business, e.g., market position, earnings, sales growth, etc.

Fungible: Possessing such a nature that one unit may be exchanged or substituted for another unit to satisfy an obligation.

Future value: $FV = PV \times (1 + i)^n$, where "FV" is future value, "PV" is present value, "i" is the assumed interest rate and "n" is the number of years.

Futures contracts: Agreements to deliver or accept commodities at stated prices on a specified future date.

Goodwill: The residual purchase price in a business acquisition that is not assignable to other identifiable assets.

Great Depression: The period of great economic hardship in the U.S. during the 1930s that followed the stock-market crash of 1929.

Gross of fees: Before fees are subtracted.

Growth, stocks: Companies whose stock trades at P/E ratios well above the market average due to accelerating earnings and who typically pay little or no dividends.

Hedge: To protect against loss by counterbalancing one transaction against another.

Hedge fund: An investment vehicle that engages in hedging as an investment strategy, often using large amounts of leverage.

High-water mark: The level of return in a hedge fund that must be exceeded before a performance-based fee may be earned.

High-yield bonds: Debt instruments that have below-investment-grade credit ratings and compensate investors with a higher coupon, or yield.

Highest-in, first-out (HIFO): A cost-flow assumption that minimizes current capital-gains tax by assuming that the highest cost shares are sold first.

Home-equity loan: A loan taken out by a homeowner against the value of the home, often in addition to the first mortgage. The interest on such loans is usually tax-deductible.

Illiquid: Incapable of quick conversion to cash.

Indenture: The legal agreement that contains the terms and conditions of a debt instrument.

Individual retirement account (IRA): An account allowed under federal tax law that permits qualified amounts to compound tax-deferred. Several forms exist today including regular, Roth and education.

Initial public offering (IPO): The first issuance to the public by a corporation of its securities.

Insolvency: The condition of being unable to meet current cash obligations. In accounting, an excess of current liabilities over current assets.

Institutional: Large, corporate investors in contrast to individuals.

Intangible assets: Assets that cannot be touched, e.g., goodwill, intellectual property, etc.

Interest-rate risk: The peril to debt investors inherent in the inverse relationship between general interest rates and security prices.

Inventories: The quantity and value of goods held for resale by a business.

Inverted: The shape of a yield curve that reflects higher short-term rates than long-term rates.

Investment bankers: Professionals who, for a fee, aid companies in identifying and executing strategic options like stock and debt offerings, acquisitions and mergers.

Investment grade: Bonds with a credit rating of BB or better.

Investment policy statement (IPS): A written investment plan that covers objectives, risk tolerance, constraints, performance measurement and target asset allocation.

Investment style: The sphere of competence of a money manager, typically described in terms of the asset class in which the manager specializes, e.g., small-cap value, etc.

Junior: Having rights in default or liquidation that are inferior to others. See subordinated.

Junk bonds: Debt instruments issued to finance corporate acquisitions in lieu of cash or stock.

Law of large numbers: The principle that, given a sufficient number of events, the average outcome is reasonably predictable. Also, the law of averages.

Leverage: The use of debt to magnify both risk and reward in the capital structure of a business or individual.

Linear: A curve that rises at a uniform rate.

Liquid: Capable of quick conversion to cash.

Liquidation: The sale of all the assets of a business, especially to satisfy creditors.

Liquidity: The state of being capable of quick conversion to cash.

Load funds: Mutual funds that charge sales fees upon either entry or exit.

Local exchanges: A country's forum for the buying and selling of assets, especially securities.

Logizomechanophobia: The fear of numerically regulated machines including computers.

Long-term debt: Borrowings that have maturities in excess of one year.

Major exchange: A large, national forum for buying and selling securities, e.g., The New York Stock Exchange or NASDAQ in the U.S.

Management accounting: The area of accounting concerned with the production of information for the managers of a business.

Margin account: A brokerage account that permits borrowing from the brokerage firm to purchase additional securities.

Margin call: A formal notice from a brokerage firm that the equity in an account must be increased to avoid liquidation of it's securities.

Marginal, tax rate: The rate at which the next dollar of income is taxed.

Market capitalization: The dollar value of all the shares of a company. It is derived by multiplying the current market price times the total number of shares outstanding.

Market makers: Dealers who stand ready to buy and sell securities in order to ensure a continuous marketplace.

Market-neutral fund: A fund that offsets each position held with a counter-position in a similar security or index.

Material, asset: Capable of being touched. See tangible.

Maturity: The length of time until a debt instrument repays its principal.

Median: The middle value in a series of numbers.

Mergers: The combination of two or more businesses into one.

Mode: The most frequently appearing value(s) in a series of numbers.

Modern portfolio theory (MPT): The seminal work on the relationship between investment risk and return. MPT is based on the synthesis of standard deviation, correlation coefficient and historical rate of return.

Mortality and expense (M&E) risk fee: An annual fee in annuity contracts, often a disguised sales fee.

Mortality tables: The statistical compilation of life expectancies upon which life insurance and lifetime annuitization are based.

Mortgage: A temporary and conditional pledge of real estate by a homeowner (mortgagor) to a lender (mortgagee) as security for the repayment of a debt.

Naked options: Option contracts wherein the writer does not own the underlying securities.

Negatively correlated: The status of two or more variables that exhibit movements in opposite patterns.

Net asset value (NAV): The per share value of a mutual fund. It is derived by dividing the market value of the fund's assets less liabilities by the number of shares.

Net income: Profits after all expenses and taxes.

Net of fees: After fees are subtracted.

Net worth: Total assets less total liabilities. See book value.

No-load funds: Mutual funds that do not charge sales fees upon either entry or exit.

Nominal rate: The stated interest rate on a debt instrument.

Open-end: An investment company with unrestricted capitalization that permits entrance of new investors; a mutual fund.

Open outcry: Based on sending and receiving instructions by human voice as opposed to computers.

Optimum: Most advantageous because the highest return is achieved for an acceptable level of risk.

Option writer: The party to an option contract who collects the premium and accepts the risk.

Outstanding: Shares of a corporation that, after issuance, remain in the hands of investors.

Passing the hat: The assessment by a partnership of an additional, proportionate contribution from the partners to their capital accounts.

Peer group: A set of investment managers whose investment style is similar.

Performance presentation standards (PPS): The calculation and presentation of investment performance data set forth by AIMR.

PITY: Price inverse to yield.

Policy: A written insurance contract.

Policyholder: The party who contracts with the insurer, usually the owner.

Portfolio: An itemized list of the assets owned by an individual or institutional investor.

Positively correlated: The status of two or more variables that exhibit movements in the same patterns.

Premium, bonds: The amount for which a bond trades above its face amount.

Premium, equities: The state of a stock that trades at a higher P/E ratio than its benchmark or relevant index.

Premium, life insurance: The payments, often in installments, for a life-insurance policy or annuity contract set forth in the agreement.

Premium, options: The payment to the option writer set forth in the option contract.

Prepayments: Expenses such as an insurance premium or rent that have been paid to others for future services to be rendered within the year.

Present value: $PV = FV[1/(1 + i)^n]$, where "PV" is present value, "FV" is future value, " i" is the assumed interest rate and "n" is the number of years.

Price/earnings (P/E) ratio: The market value per share of a stock divided by its annual earnings per share. See earnings multiple.

Principal: A sum of money owed as a debt on which interest is computed.

Private mortgage insurance (PMI): Insurance on the life of the borrower for the benefit of the lender that adds to the monthly cost of a mortgage; typically, PMI is required when the homeowner borrows more than 80% of a property's value.

Profit: The annual earnings of a business that results from subtracting expenses from revenues.

Prospectus: A formal, written summary of a stock, debt or mutual-fund offering to the public. Its contents and form are governed by SEC guidelines.

Public company: A corporation whose shares are traded freely in contrast to a private business.

Put option: A contract that entitles the owner to sell, or put, securities at a set price for a specified period of time.

Real rate: The nominal or stated rate less inflation.

Realized gains: Gains that have been obtained through a sale in contrast to paper gains.

Rebalancing: The act of periodically restoring the target percentages in each asset class contained in a portfolio.

Recapitalizations: The retooling of a company's capital structure.

Reciprocal: The quotient of a value divided into one. For example, the reciprocal of 8 is 1/8.

Recourse notes: Borrowings that permit the lender to assess the borrower personally in the event of default.

Redemption fees: Fees imposed by a mutual fund company on investors who withdraw from the fund family within a specified time period.

Regressing to the mean: The tendency of investment results, given sufficient time, to resemble the historical average results.

Reinvestment fees: Fees imposed by a mutual-fund company on investors who reinvest fund distributions in the same fund family.

Reinvestment risk: The possibility that interest and principal payments on debt instruments cannot be reinvested at as favorable a yield.

Relative: The value of a quantity expressed as a percentage of another value, e.g., absolute variability divided by the population average.

Research and development (R&D): The costs associated with scientific inquiry to improve existing products and services and to develop new ones.

Reserves: An amount of capital held back from investment to meet probable future demands.

Retained earnings: The undistributed, accumulated profits of a business.

Retiring: Extinguishing debt by paying it off.

Return on assets (ROA): The quotient derived by dividing the annual profits of a business by the average total assets.

Return on equity (ROE): The quotient derived by dividing the annual profits of a business by the average shareholders' equity.

Revenue: The accounting term for sales or shipments expressed in dollars.

Reverse mortgage: A contract wherein the homeowner receives a monthly check in exchange for surrendering equity in the home.

Risk premium: Any return in excess of the risk-free rate.

Roll over: To effect a qualified tax-free exchange with an annuity or IRA.

Russell 2000 index: A stock-market index that primarily includes small-cap and micro-cap companies with market capitalizations under $1 billion.

Seasoned: Debt securities that trade in the secondary market subsequent to their initial offering.

Secondary market: The market for securities that have already been purchased by the public.

Secondary offering: Any public offering of stock that follows the issuer's initial public offering.

Security, debts: The borrower's assets or revenue streams that serve as the backing for interest and debt repayment.

Senior: Having rights in default or liquidation that are superior to others.

Shadow stocks: Stocks neglected by Wall Street analysts.

Shareholder return: The return of a mutual fund associated with an investment that is subject to the contributions and withdrawals of the investor.

Short sale: The sale of borrowed shares.

Short squeeze: The excess demand and resultant rising prices brought about by short sellers seeking to cover their positions.

Simple interest: Interest that is calculated on principal only.

Sisyphean: Suggestive of the labors of Sisyphus, the legendary Corinthian king, whose vain attempts to roll a rock to the top of a hill in Hades remain a symbol of futility.

Slide error: A mistake caused by the misplacement of the decimal point in a number.

Socially responsible fund: A fund that uses an increasingly popular investment approach that excludes companies whose businesses violate investors' values, e.g., animal testing or weapons manufacturing, and includes companies whose practices support investors' values, e.g., workforce diversity and positive environmental programs.

Solvent: Capable of meeting current cash obligations.

Spam: Unwanted E-mail touting products and services. The equivalent of junk mail through the postal system.

Speculating: Engaging in risky investments in the hope of quick or considerable profits.

Spin-offs: The disposition of a division or line of business by a company.

Spread: The difference between the price demanded and the price offered for a security.

Standard & Poor's (S&P) 500 index: A market-cap-weighted index of 500 representative, large-cap companies.

Standard deviation: The statistical measure of dispersion in a set of values.

Strike price: The set price in an option contract.

Style drift: A marked deviation from a money manager's stated investment approach.

Subaccounts: The investment choices within a variable annuity.

Subordinated: Having rights in default or liquidation that are inferior to others. See junior.

Surrender: To permit an insurance policy to expire.

Syndicators: The organizers and marketers of a limited partnership.

Systematic risk: Risk that is attributable to the market in general as opposed to a security in particular.

Tangible, asset: Capable of being touched. See material.

Target-maturity debt: Debt instruments and funds whose maturity can be matched to the investor's need for cash.

Tax-deferred: Permitting the postponement of taxes into the future.

Tax-equivalent yield: The taxable yield that corresponds to a stated tax-exempt yield.

Tax-exempt: The status of interest on municipal debt that is exempt from federal income taxes.

Tax-free exchange: An annuity or insurance-policy exchange that does not trigger taxes.

Technical, analysis: Security analysis based on factors that are extrinsic to a business, e.g., stock-price trends, institutional ownership, trading volume, short interest, etc.

Thin: The market condition caused by a limited number of buyers and sellers.

Ticker symbol: The market shorthand for a security.

Tilt: The investment classification of a stock or mutual fund, especially growth or value.

Top-down: An approach to security analysis that primarily looks at macroeconomic data and trends.

Total return: The measure of performance that includes both price change and income.

Training-wheel fund: A simplified fund with a low investment requirement for novice investors.

Transposition error: A mistake caused by the exchanging of two consecutive digits in a number.

Triple tax-exempt: The status of interest on municipal debt that is exempt from federal, state and local income taxes.

Turnover: The quotient expressed as a percentage of annual security sales divided by the average portfolio value. The measure of trading activity within a portfolio.

Uncorrelated: The status of two or more variables that exhibit movements in random patterns.

Underwriting: The business of guaranteeing the purchase of a full issue of stock or bonds.

Unified credit: The lifetime transfer-tax credit available to a U.S. taxpayer.

Uniform Transfer to Minors Act (UTMA): A state law that permits the opening of custodial accounts for the benefit of a minor, usually under 18 or 21 years of age.

Universe: The global set of securities available.

Unrealized, gains: Gains that have not yet been obtained through a sale. Also, paper gains.

Unsystematic risk: Risk that is attributable to a security in particular as opposed to the market in general.

Value, stocks: Companies whose stock trades at P/E ratios well below the market average due to cyclical or flat earnings and who typically pay high, steady dividends.

Variability: The degree of dispersion in a set of asset values or returns over time.

Viator: A life-insurance policy owner who assigns the policy's death benefit to a purchaser in exchange for immediate cash.

Volatility: See variability.

Wall Street: The street at the bottom of Manhattan in New York City that has long been the locus of the U.S. securities industry.

Weighted average: An average derived after assigning weights to the members of a set that indicate the relative importance of each member's contribution to the result.

Working capital: In accounting, current assets less current liabilities.

Wrap programs: A sales approach in which all investment advice and brokerage commissions are included in a single annual fee.

Yield, debt: The annual coupon of a debt instrument divided by the current market price.

Yield-to-maturity: The yield that considers both the coupon and any capital gain or loss attributable to a discount or premium that will be realized at maturity.

Index

A

Amazon.com, 106
American Association of Individual
    Investors, 100
American Institute of Certified Public
    Accountants, 22
Apple Computer, 112
Association of Investment Mgmt. and
    Research, 97

B

Beardstown Ladies, 126, 133
Beloit Corporation, 119
Best, A.M., 47, 74, 94
Big Mac index, 103
Bogle, John, 84
Borders Group, 106
Bowie, David, 56
Buffett, Warren, 38, 57

C

Cendant Corp., 23
Central Registration Depository, 93
Chock Full O' Nuts, 108
Chrysler, 15
Coca-Cola, 23, 117, 118

D

Daimler-Benz, 15
Department of Labor Statistics, 12
Diogenes of Sinope, 92
Domini, Amy (Domini social index), 136
Dow Chemical, 113, 114, 115
Dow Dogs, 85

E

eBay, Inc., 109
Economic value added, 117
Ehrbar, Al, 119

F

FDIC, 46
Federal National Mortgage
    Association, 53
Federal Reserve Bank, 4, 103
Federal Witness Protection Program, 93
Fidelity Magellan, 86
Financial Accounting Standards Board, 22
First Call, 109
Franklin, Benjamin, 168
Franklin Resources, 85

G

Gates, Bill, 18
Generally accepted accounting
    principles, 22, 23, 29, 31, 57, 113,
    117, 118
The Giant Spider Invasion, 77
Government National Mortgage
    Association, 53
Graham and Dodd, 111
Greenspan, Alan, 103

H

Halley, Edmond, 49
Harley-Davidson, 107
Harnischfeger Industries, 119
Home Depot, 111

I

IBM, 116
Intel, 23, 117
Investment Company Act of 1940, 85
IRS, 14, 47, 72, 89, 164

J

Johnson, Ned, 84

K

Kmart, 107, 119